FOR ORGANS, PIANOS & ELECTRONIC KEYBOARDS

E-Z PLAY® TODAY

375

THE SONGS OF
Bacharach & David

T0034072

CONTENTS

ISBN 978-0-634-01147-4

HAL•LEONARD®
CORPORATION

7777 W. BLUEMOUND RD. P.O. BOX 13819 MILWAUKEE, WI 53213

E-Z PLAY ® TODAY Music Notation © 1975 by HAL LEONARD CORPORATION

E-Z PLAY and EASY ELECTRONIC KEYBOARD MUSIC are registered trademarks of HAL LEONARD CORPORATION.

Visit Hal Leonard Online at
www.halleonard.com

Alfie
Theme from the Paramount Picture ALFIE

Registration 9
Rhythm: 8 Beat or Pops

Words by Hal David
Music by Burt Bacharach

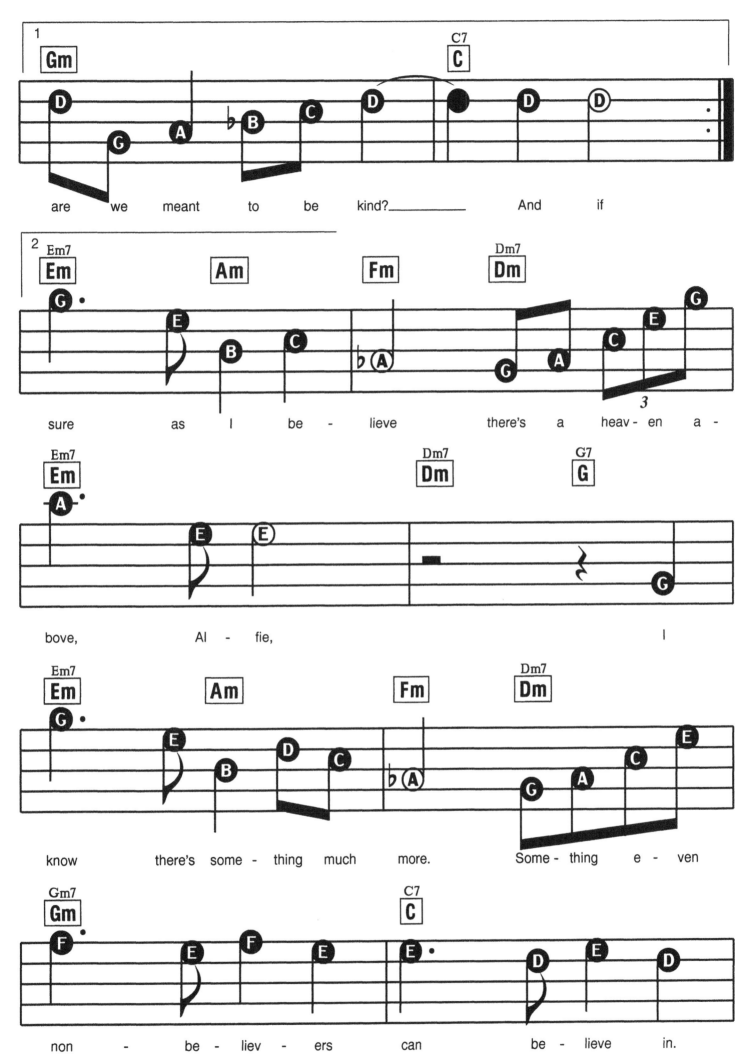

(There's)
Always Something
There to Remind Me

Registration 7
Rhythm: Rock or 8 Beat

Lyric by Hal David
Music by Burt Bacharach

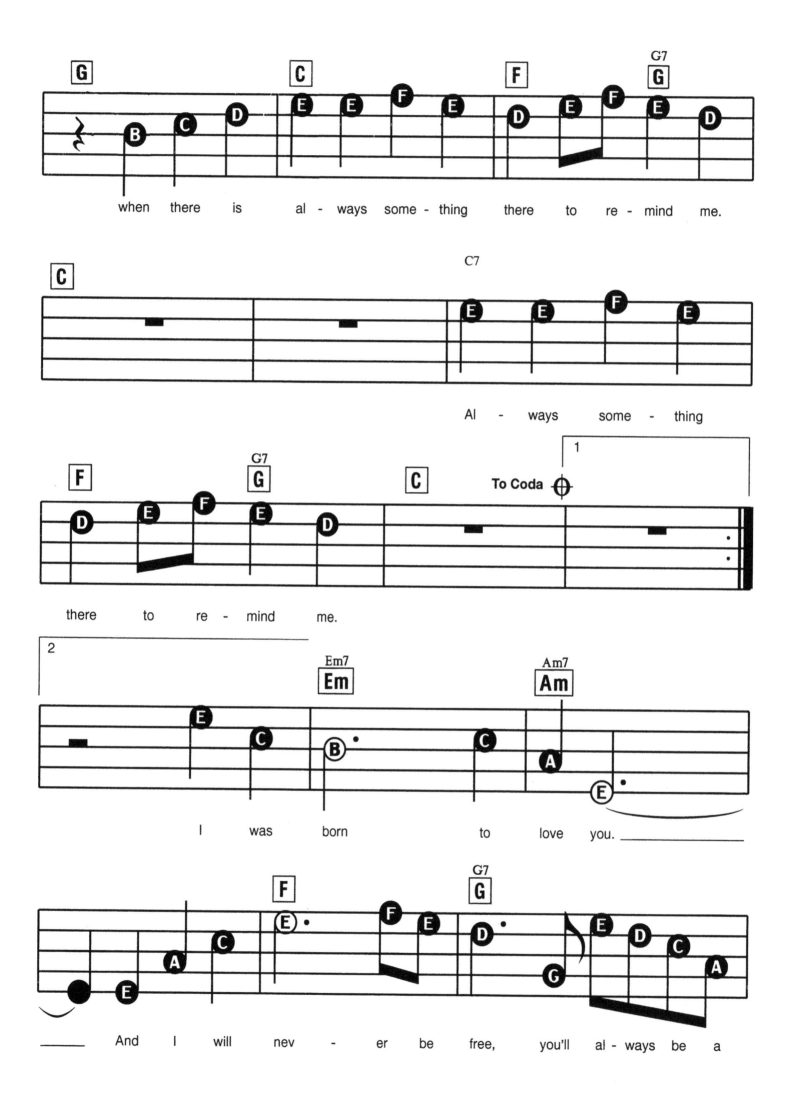

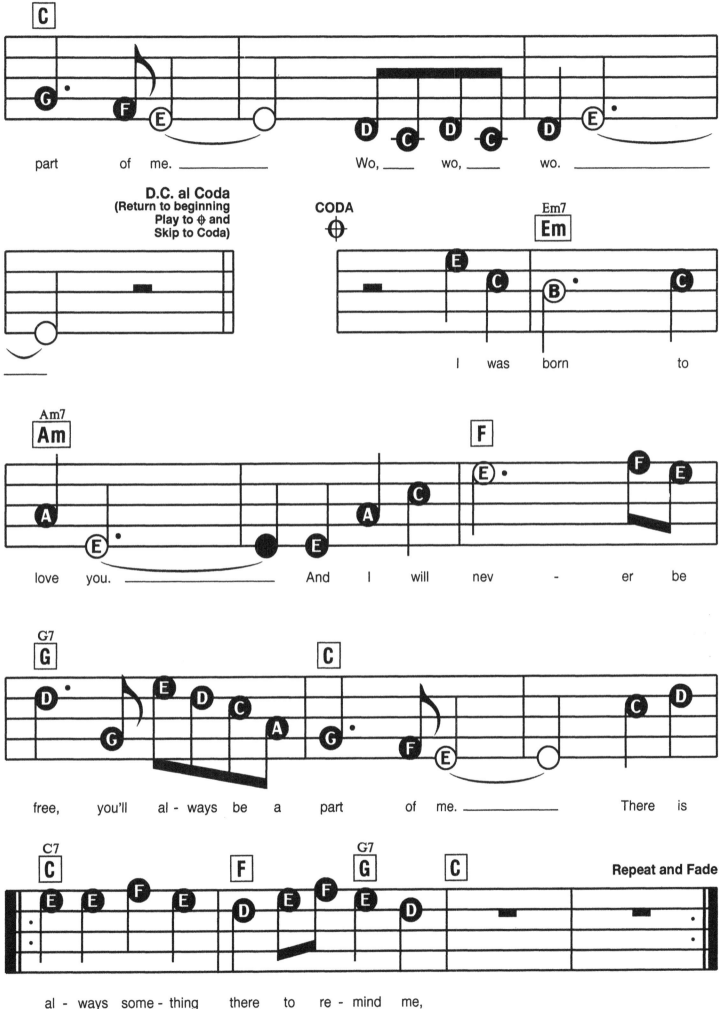

The April Fools

Registration 1
Rhythm: Ballad

Lyric by Hal David
Music by Burt Bacharach

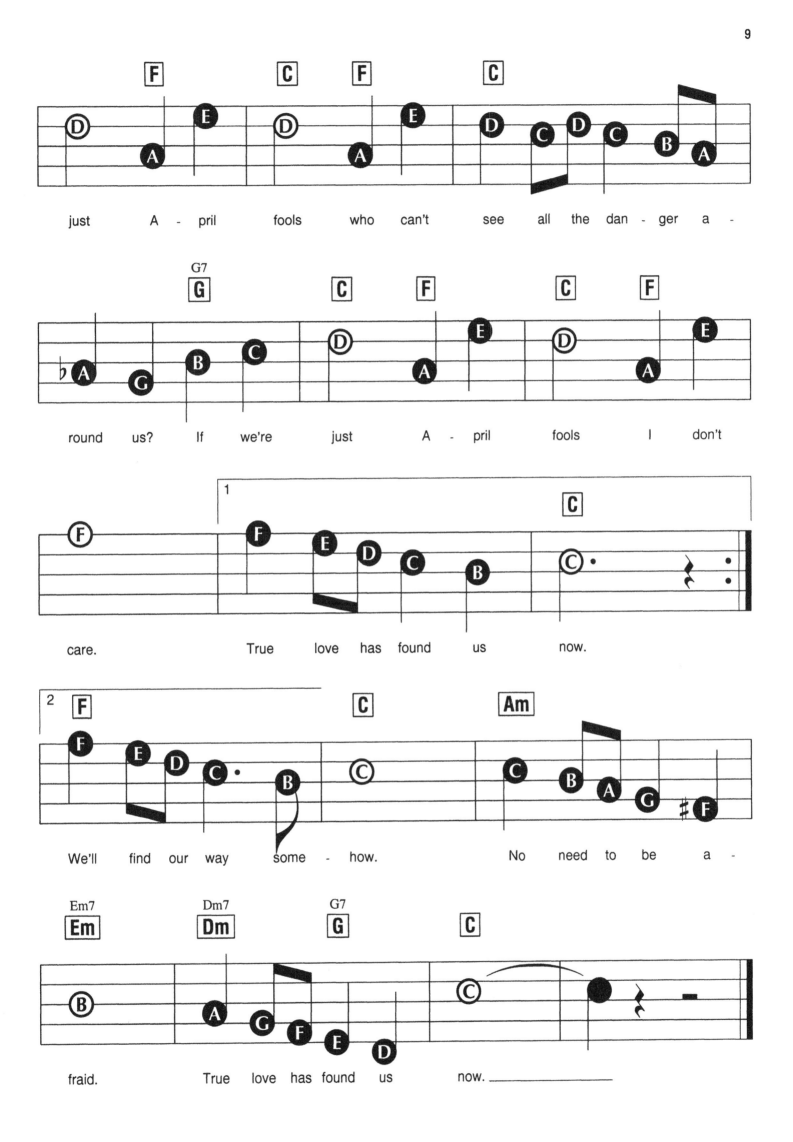

(They Long to Be)
Close to You

Registration 10
Rhythm: Swing, Shuffle, or Ballad

Lyric by Hal David
Music by Burt Bacharach

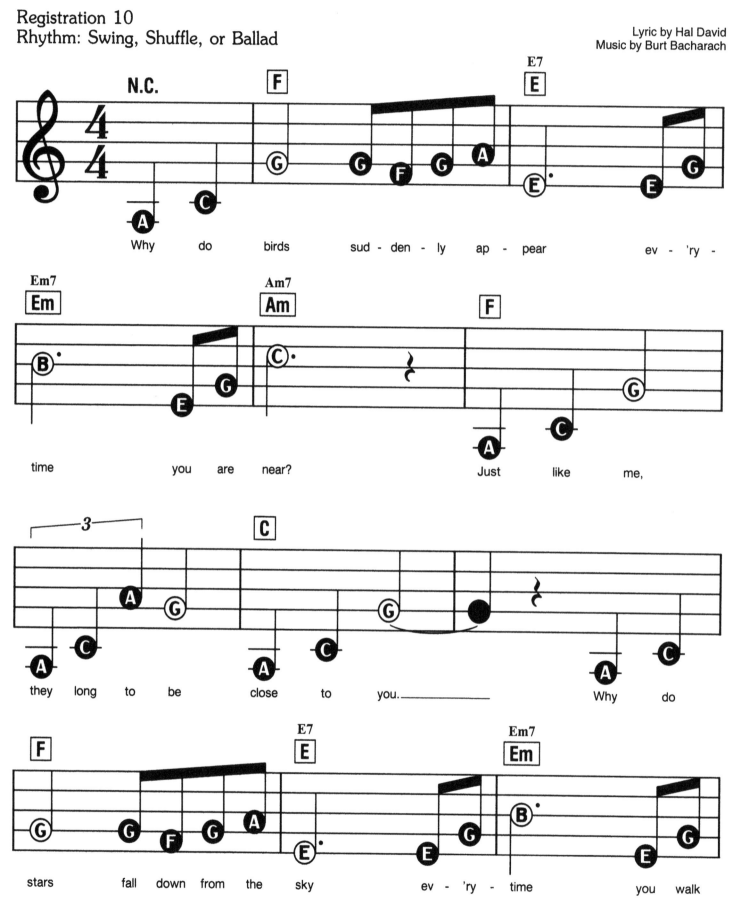

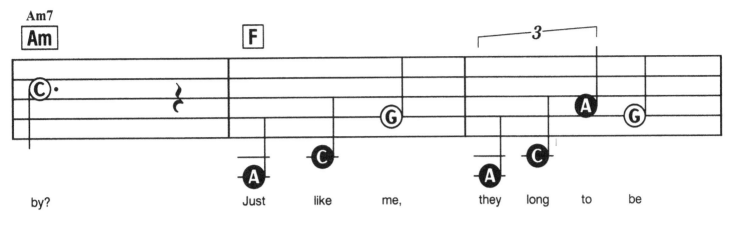

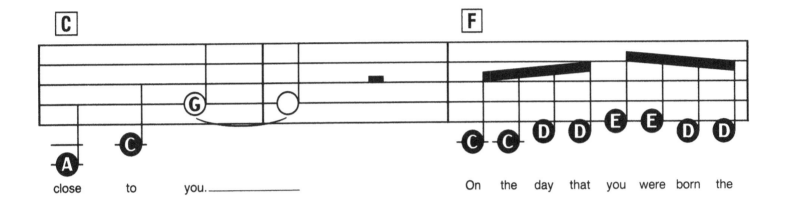

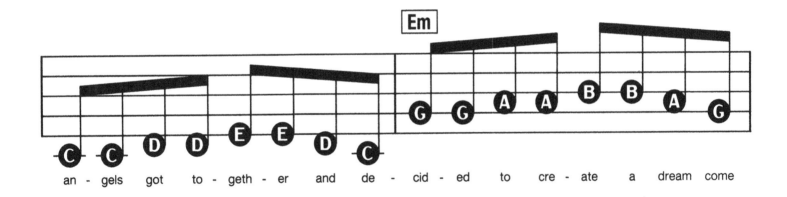

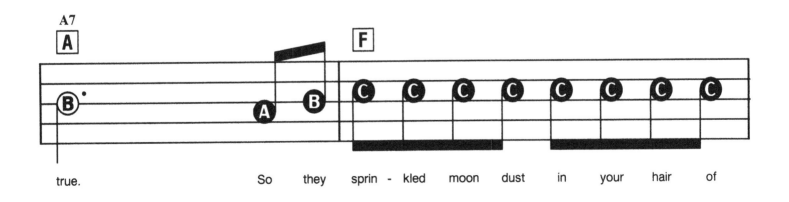

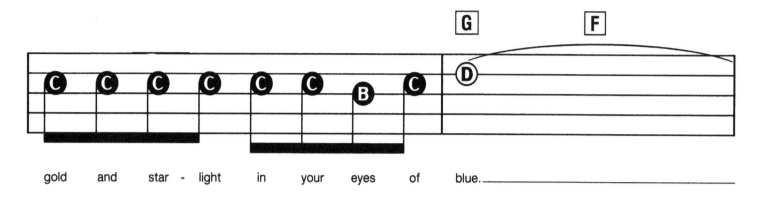

gold and star - light in your eyes of blue._____

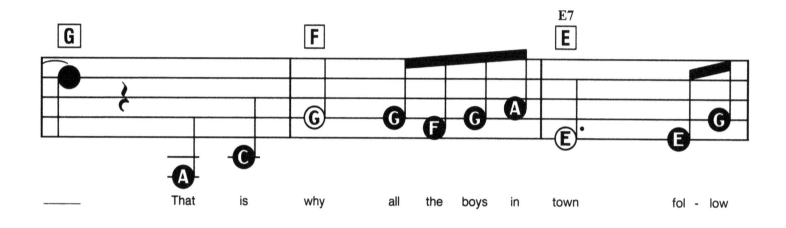

_____ That is why all the boys in town fol - low

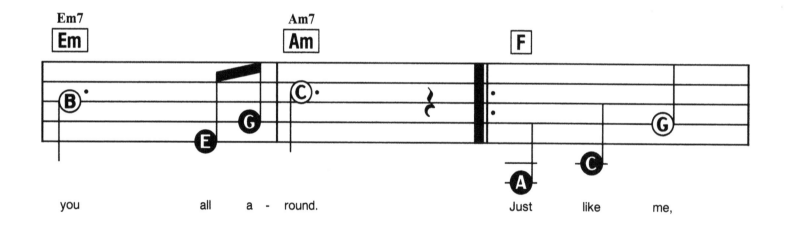

you all a - round. Just like me,

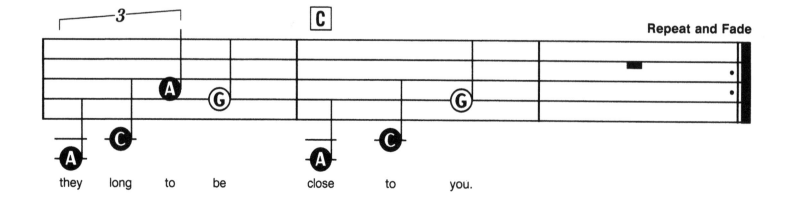

Repeat and Fade

they long to be close to you.

Do You Know the Way to San Jose

Registration 5
Rhythm: Rock or 8 Beat

Lyric by Hal David
Music by Burt Bacharach

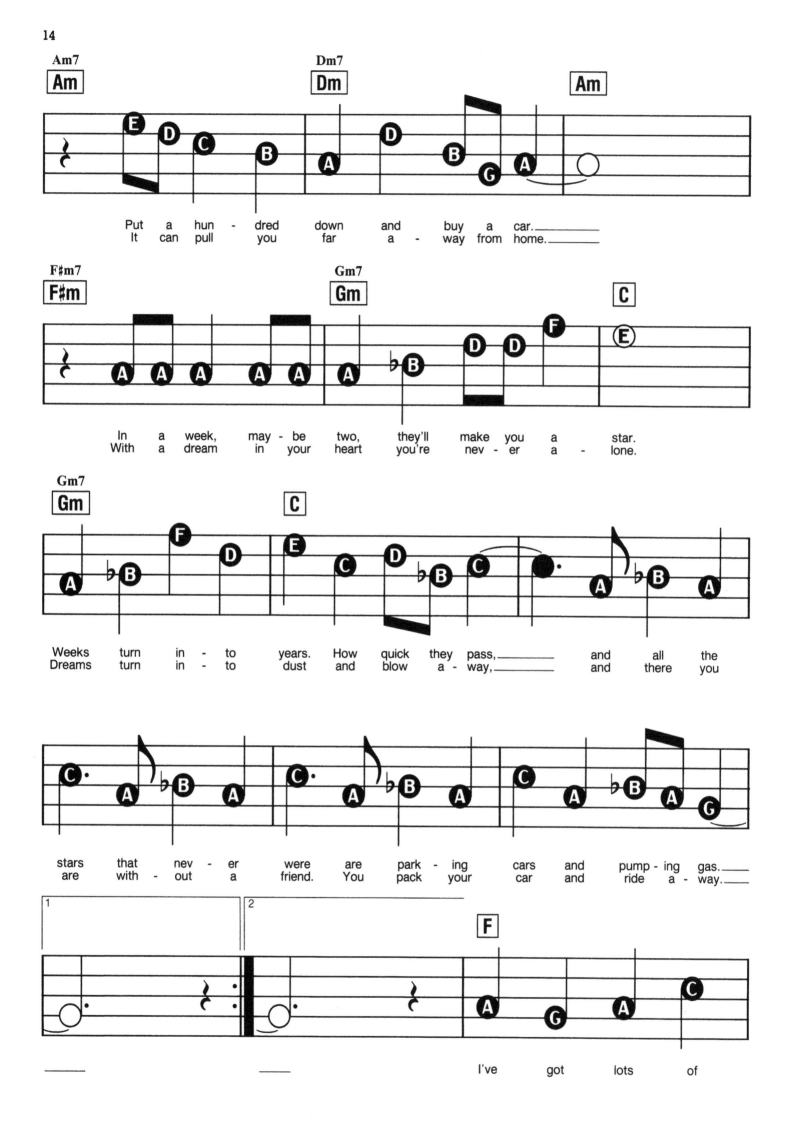

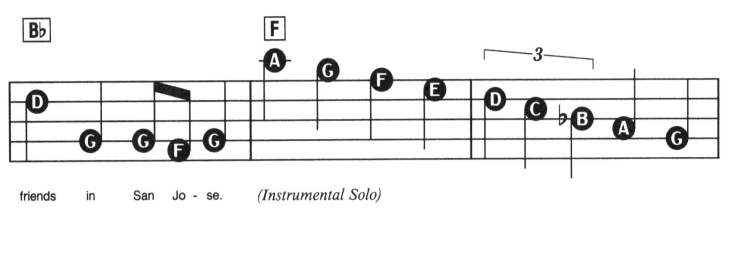

friends   in   San Jo - se.   *(Instrumental Solo)*

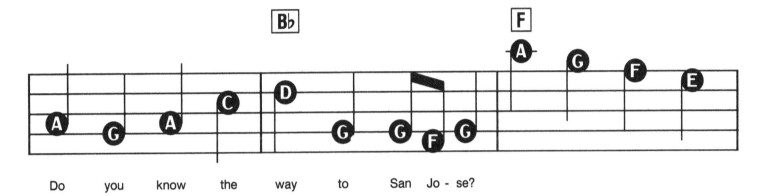

Do   you   know   the   way   to   San Jo - se?

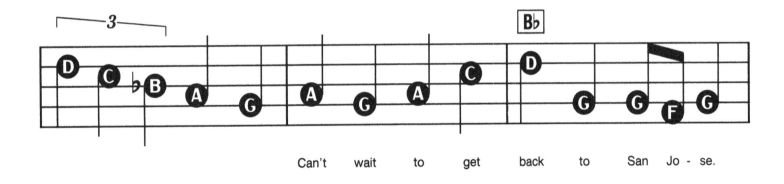

Can't   wait   to   get   back   to   San Jo - se.

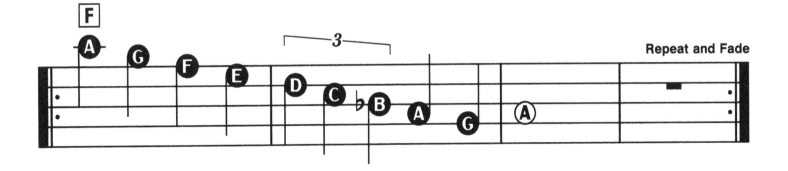

Repeat and Fade

Don't Make Me Over

Registration 1
Rhythm: Waltz

Lyric by Hal David
Music by Burt Bacharach

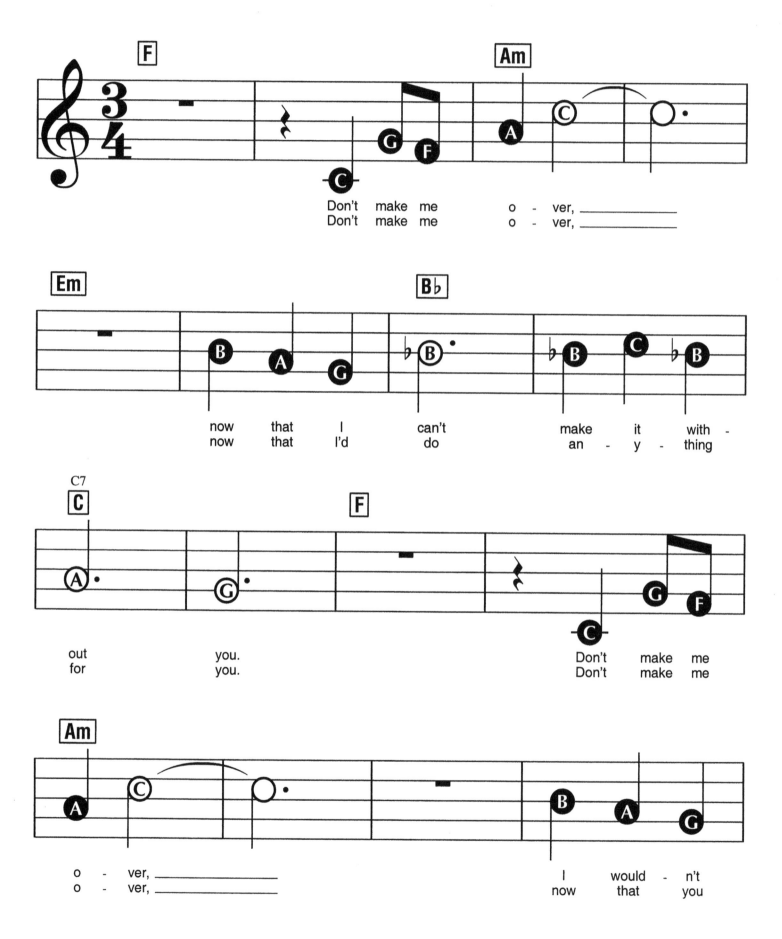

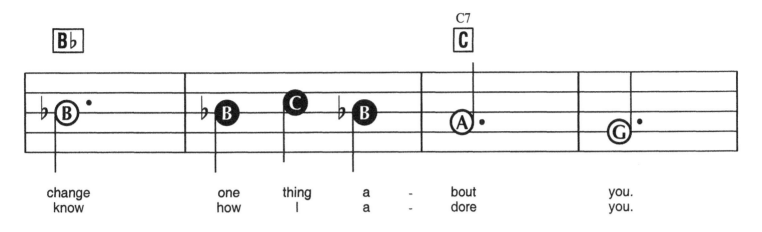

change   one   thing   a   -   bout   you.
know   how   I   a   -   dore   you.

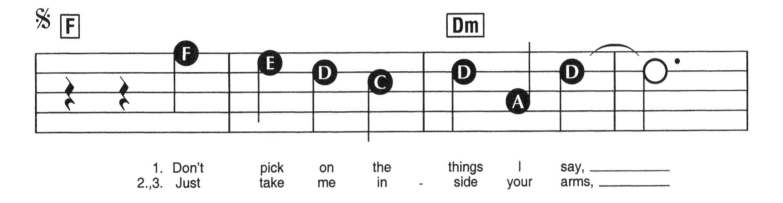

1. Don't   pick   on   the   things   I   say, _____
2.,3. Just   take   me   in   -   side   your   arms, _____

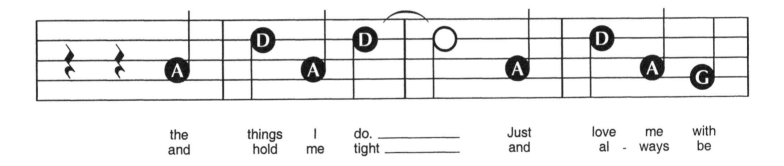

the   things   I   do. _____   Just   love   me   with
and   hold   me   tight _____   and   al   -   ways   be

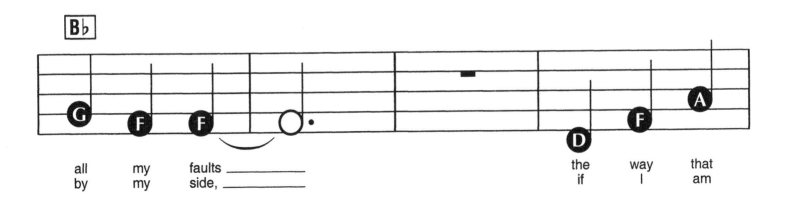

all   my   faults _____   the   way   that
by   my   side, _____   if   I   am

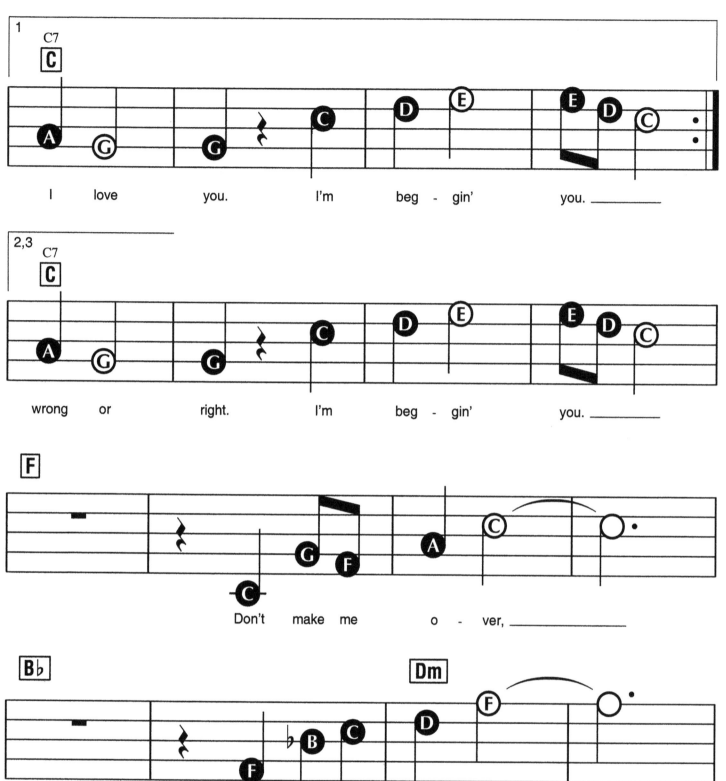

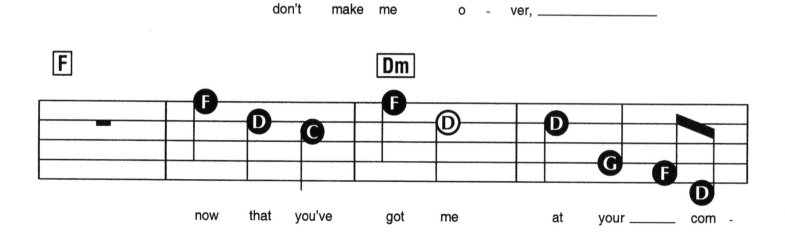

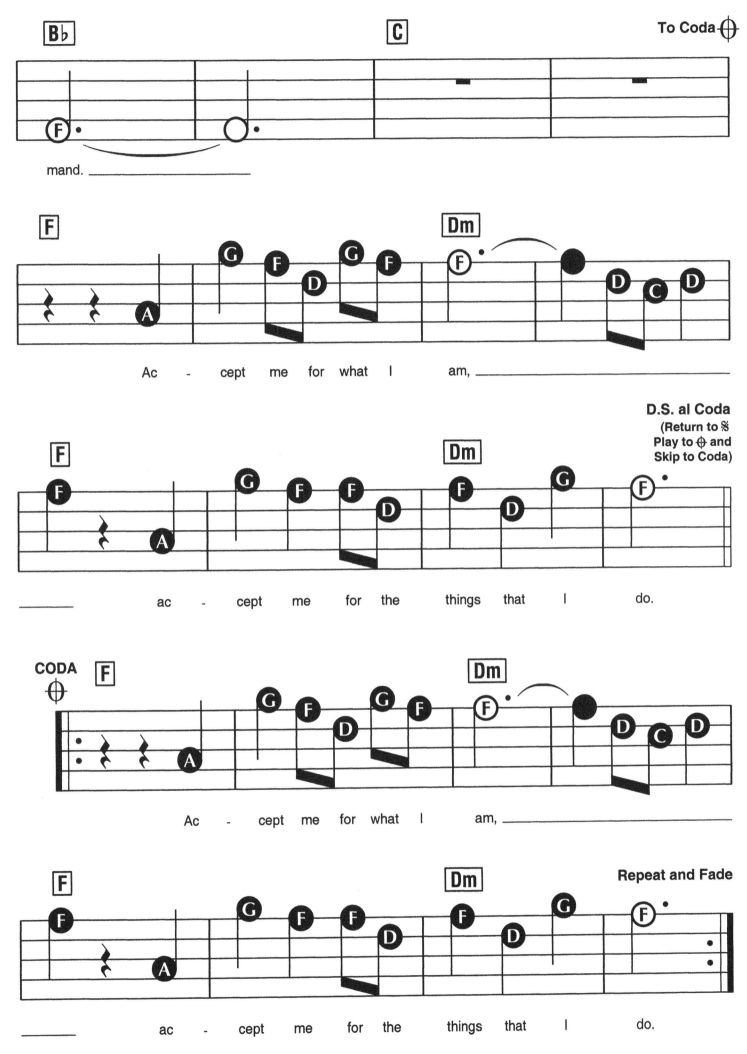

A House Is Not a Home

Registration 8
Rhythm: Ballad or Fox Trot

Lyric by Hal David
Music by Burt Bacharach

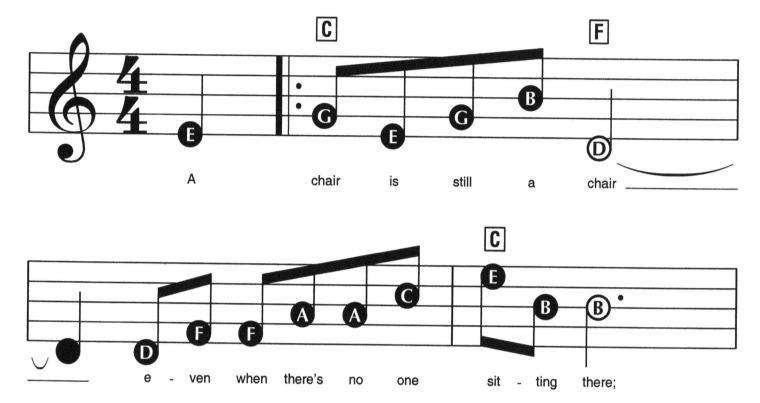

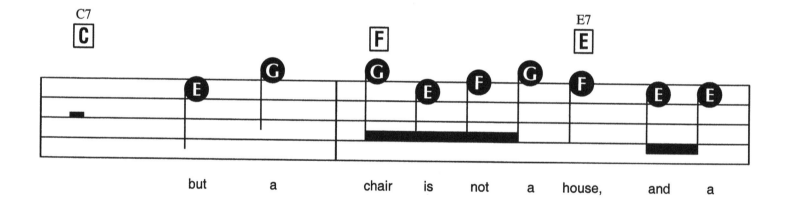

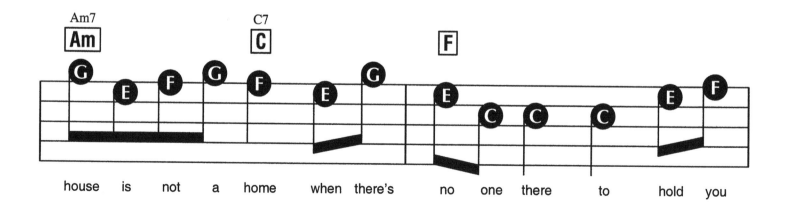

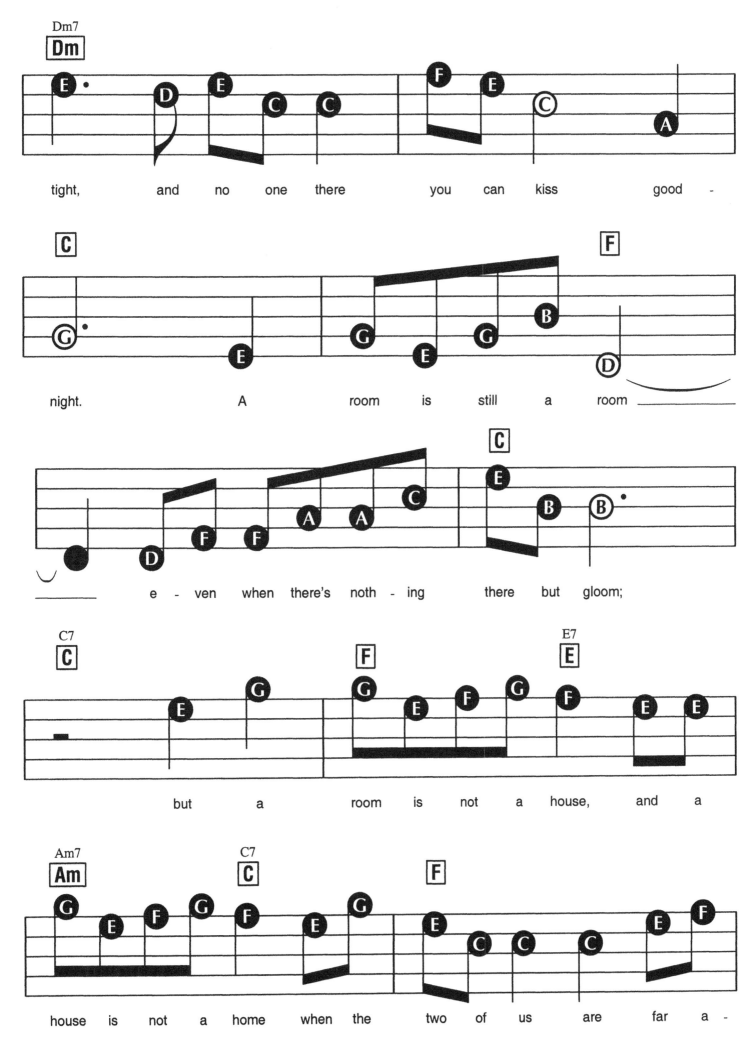

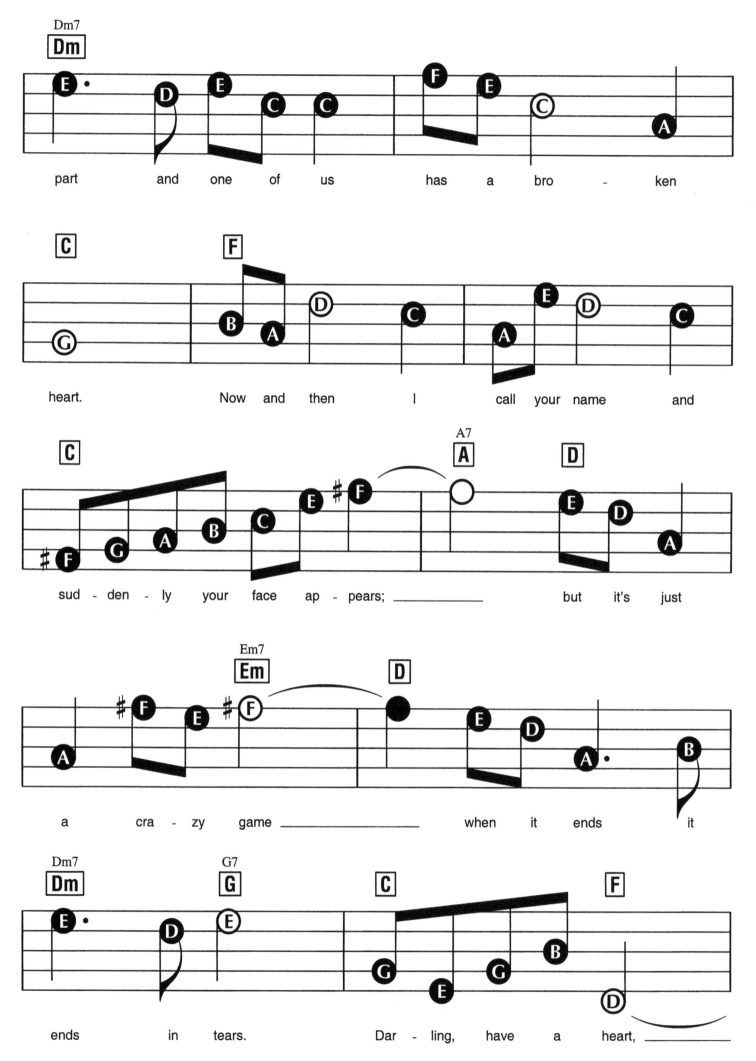

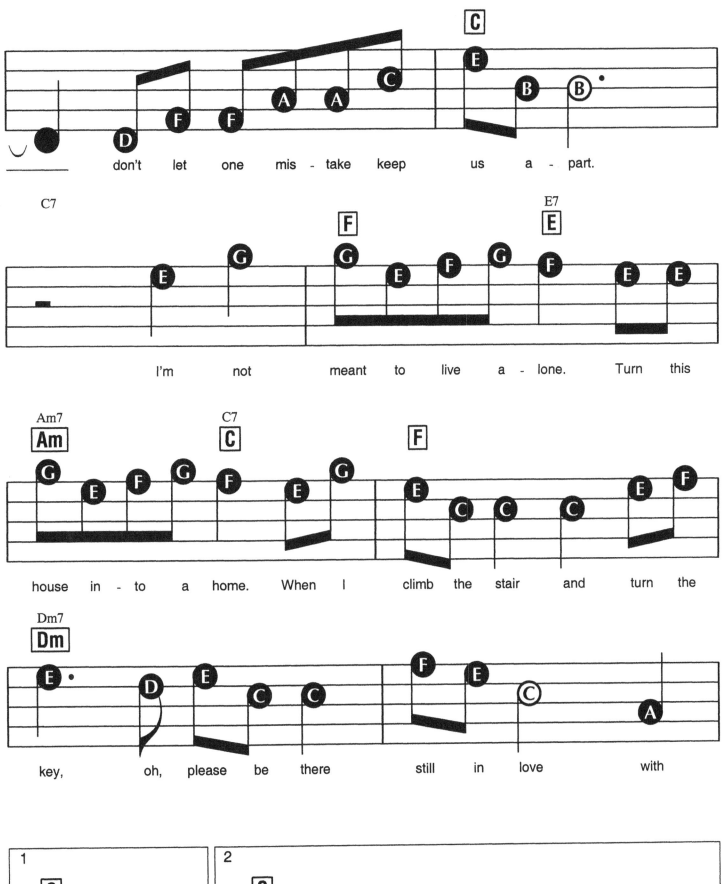
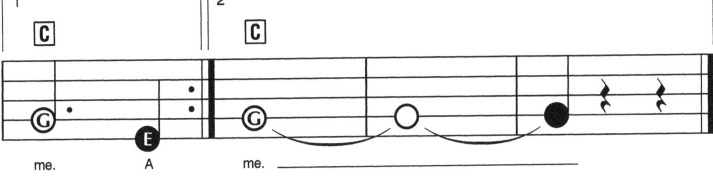

C
D F F A A C E B B
don't let one mis - take keep us a - part.
C7 F E7 E
E G G E F G F E E
I'm not meant to live a - lone. Turn this
Am7 Am C7 C F
G E F G F E G E C C C E F
house in - to a home. When I climb the stair and turn the
Dm7 Dm
E D E C C F E C A
key, oh, please be there still in love with
1 C 2 C
G E G
me. A me.

I Say a Little Prayer

Registration 7
Rhythm: Bossa Nova, Pops, or 8 Beat

Lyric by Hal David
Music by Burt Bacharach

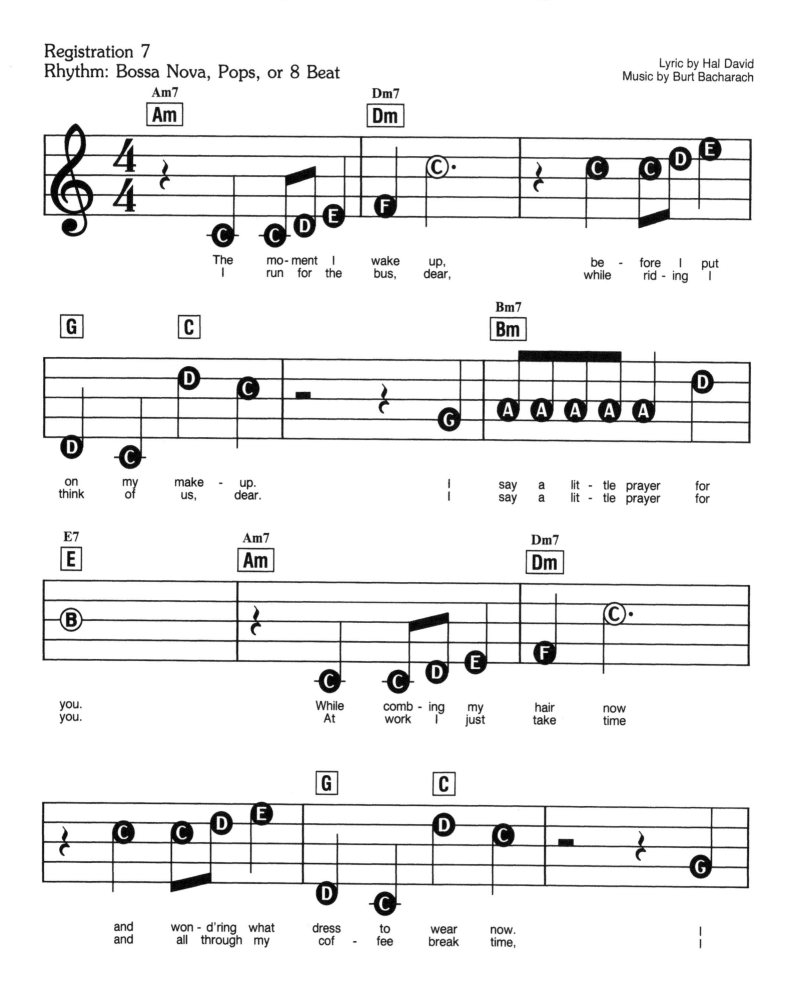

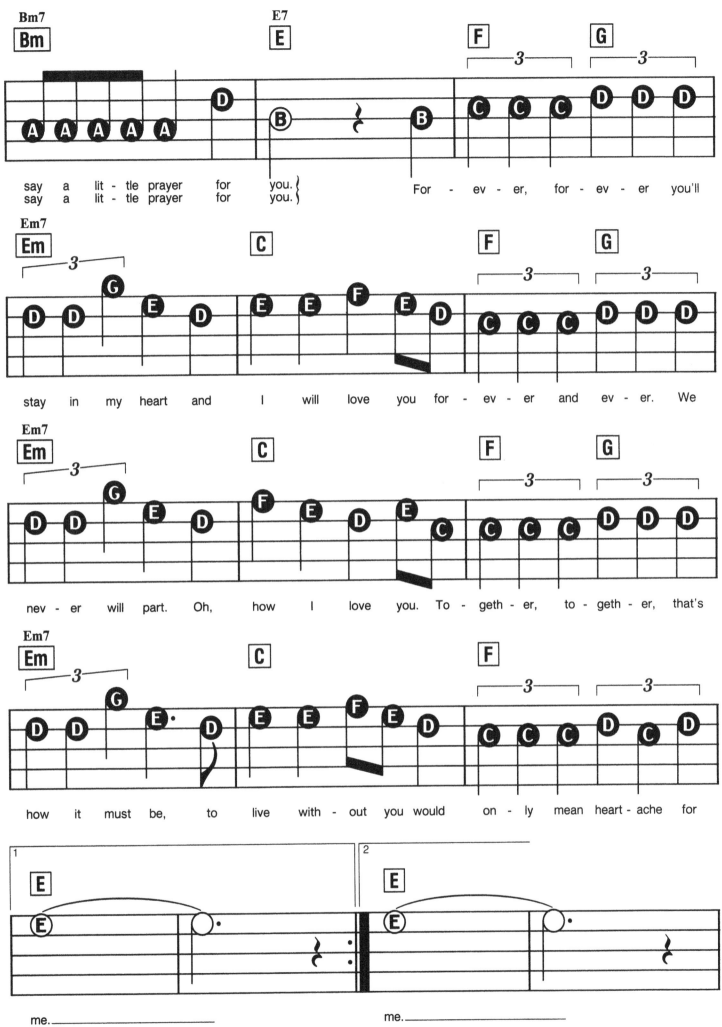

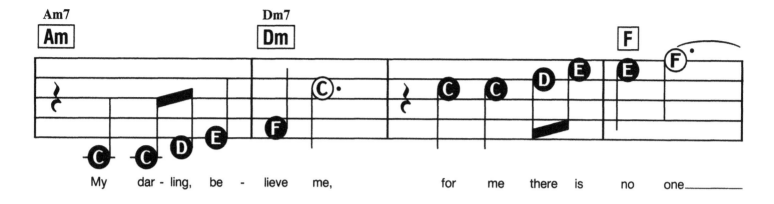

My dar - ling, be - lieve me, for me there is no one_____

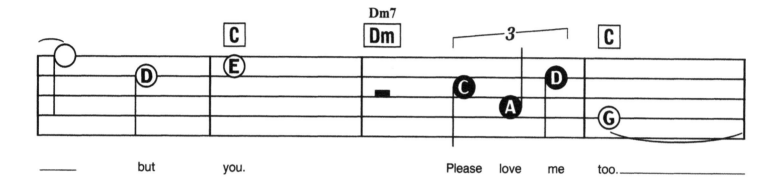

_____ but you. Please love me too._____

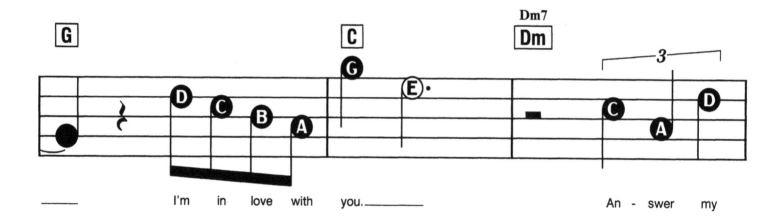

_____ I'm in love with you._____ An - swer my

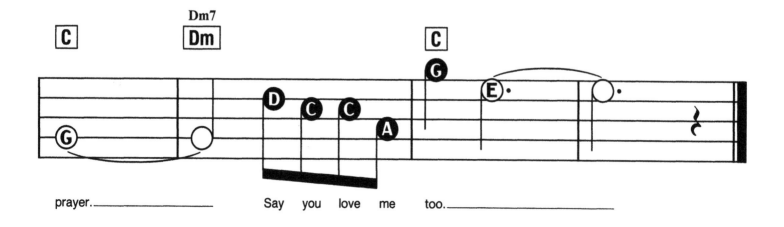

prayer._____ Say you love me too._____

Make It Easy on Yourself

Registration 7
Rhythm: Ballad or Slow Rock

Lyric by Hal David
Music by Burt Bacharach

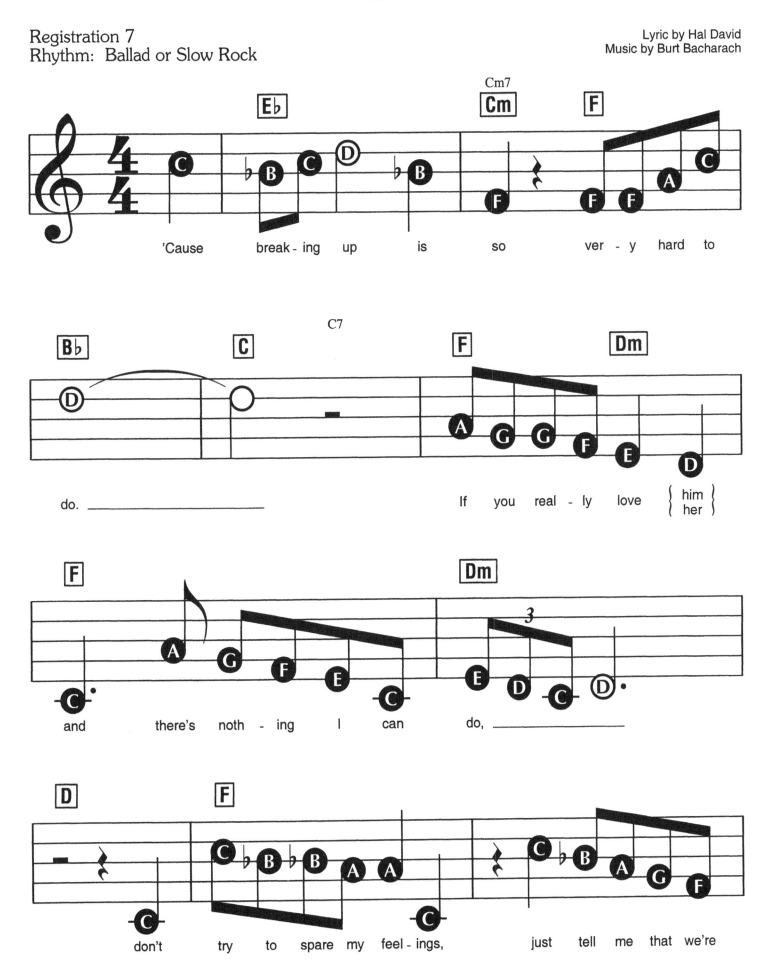

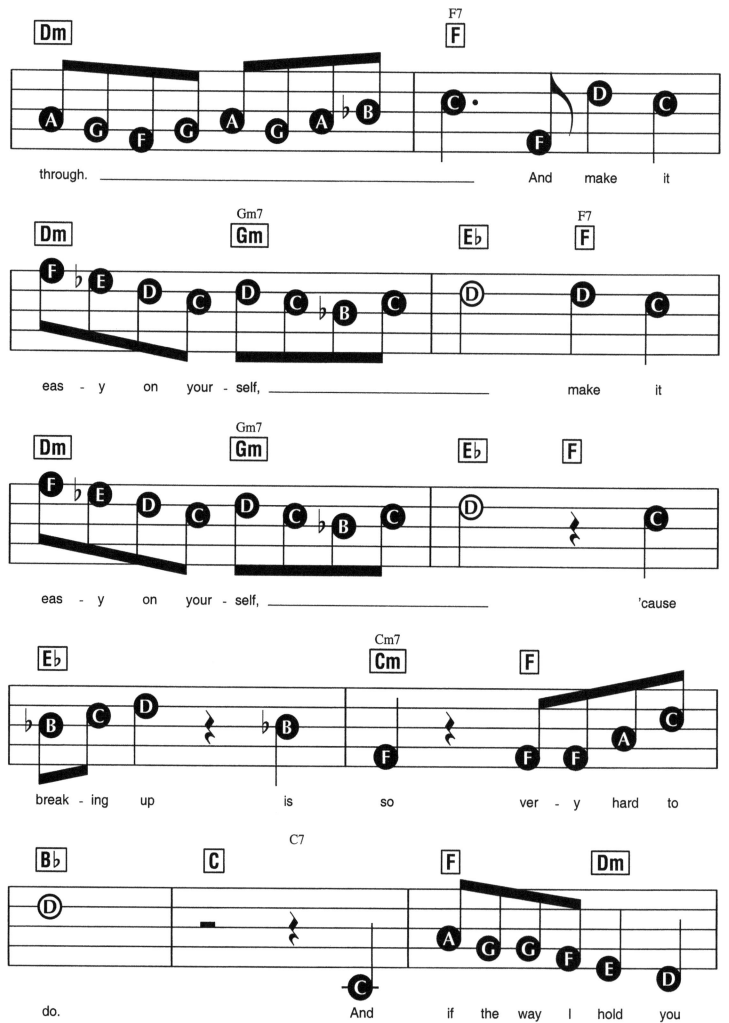

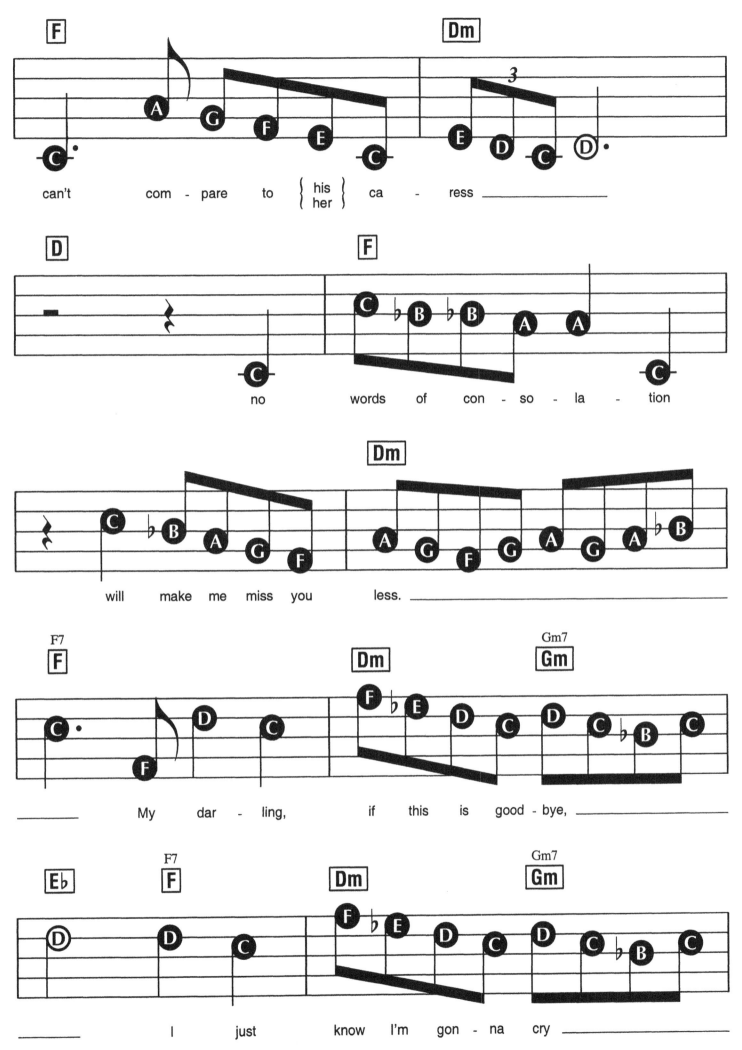

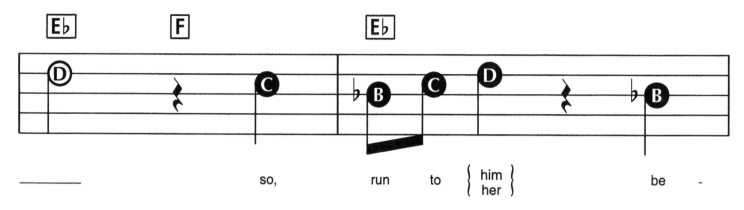

so, run to { him / her } be -

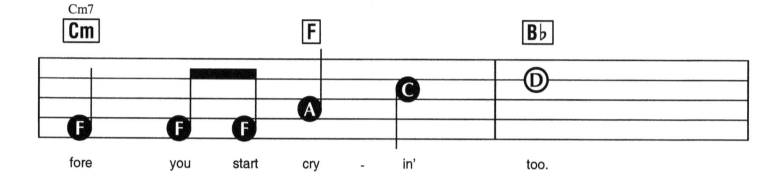

fore you start cry - in' too.

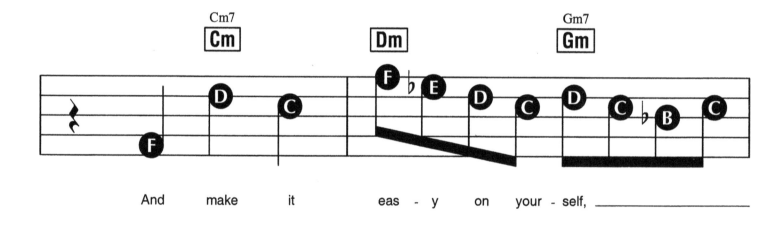

And make it eas - y on your - self, _____

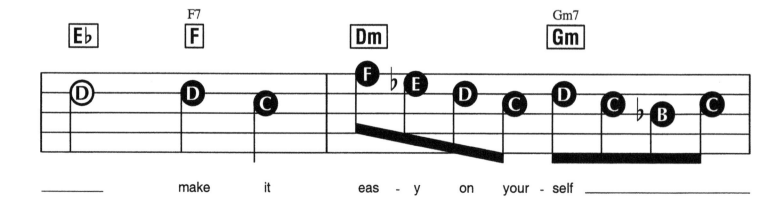

_____ make it eas - y on your - self _____

31

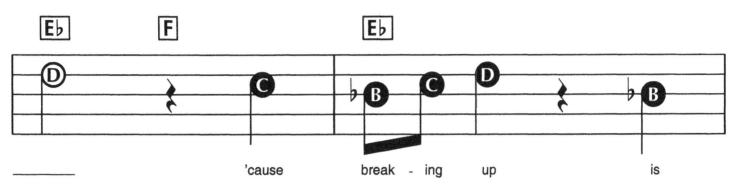

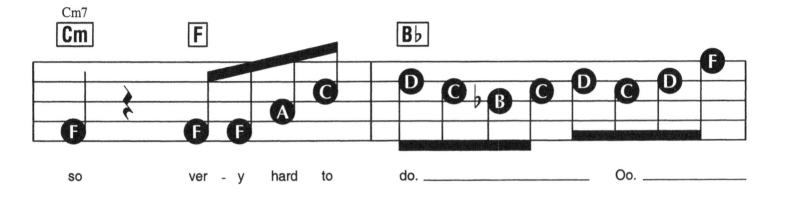

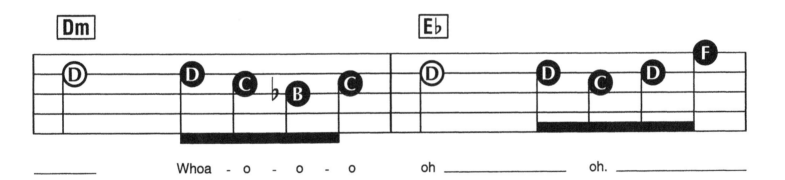

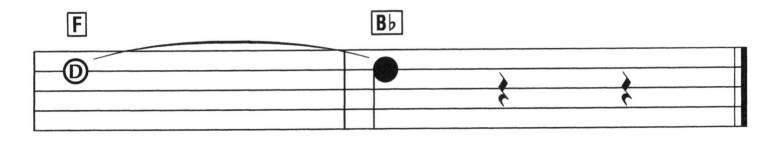

I'll Never Fall in Love Again
from PROMISES, PROMISES

Registration 1
Rhythm: Pops or Rock

Lyric by Hal David
Music by Burt Bacharach

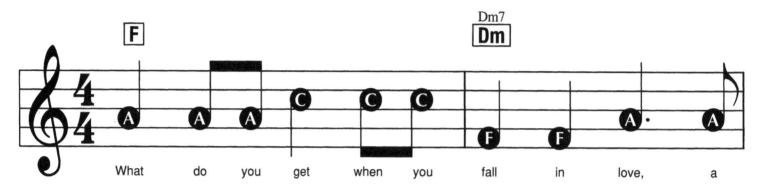

What do you get when you fall in love, a

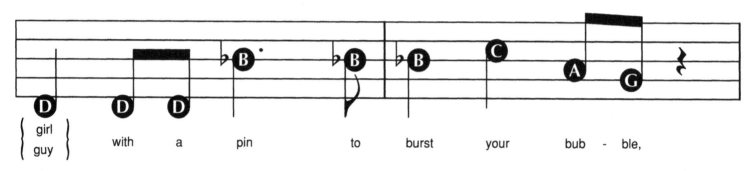

girl / guy   with a pin to burst your bub - ble,

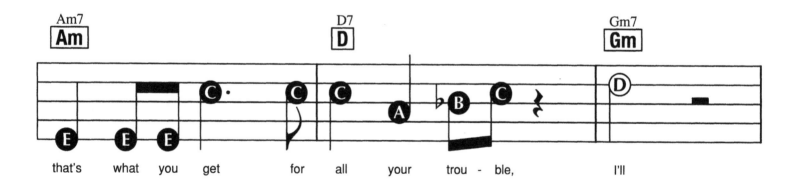

that's what you get for all your trou - ble, I'll

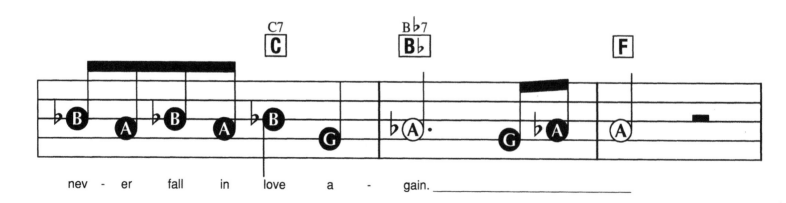

nev - er fall in love a - gain. _____

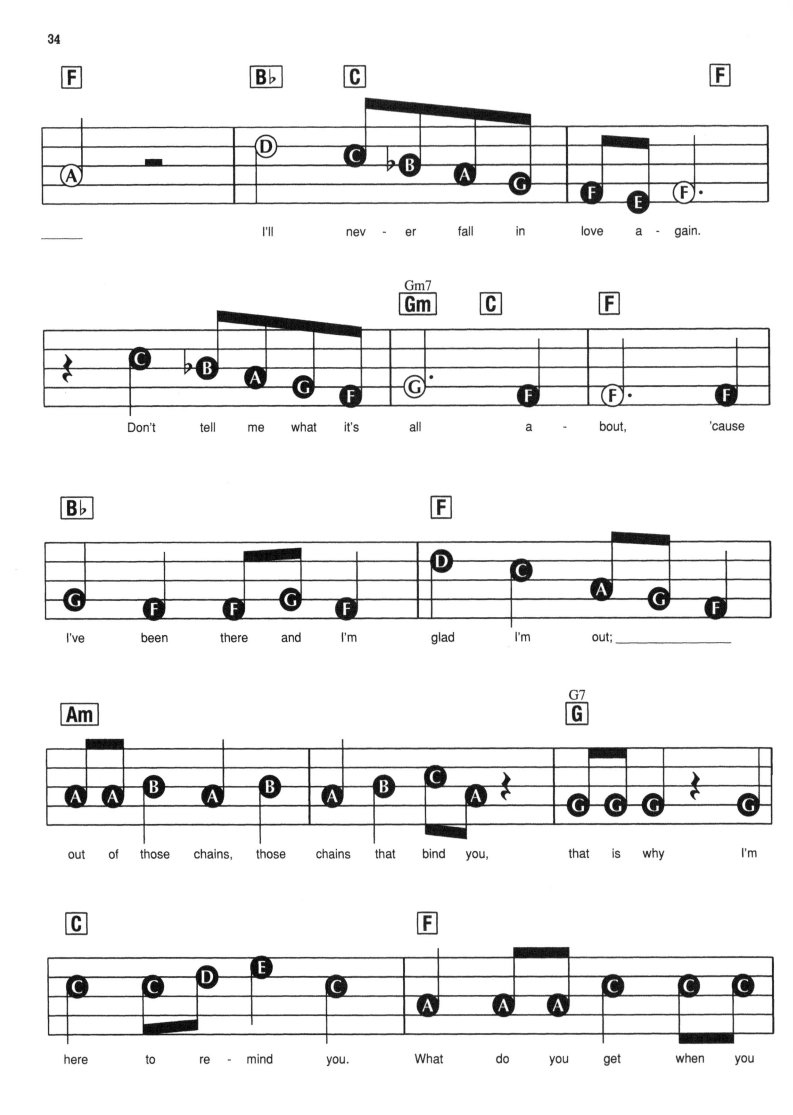

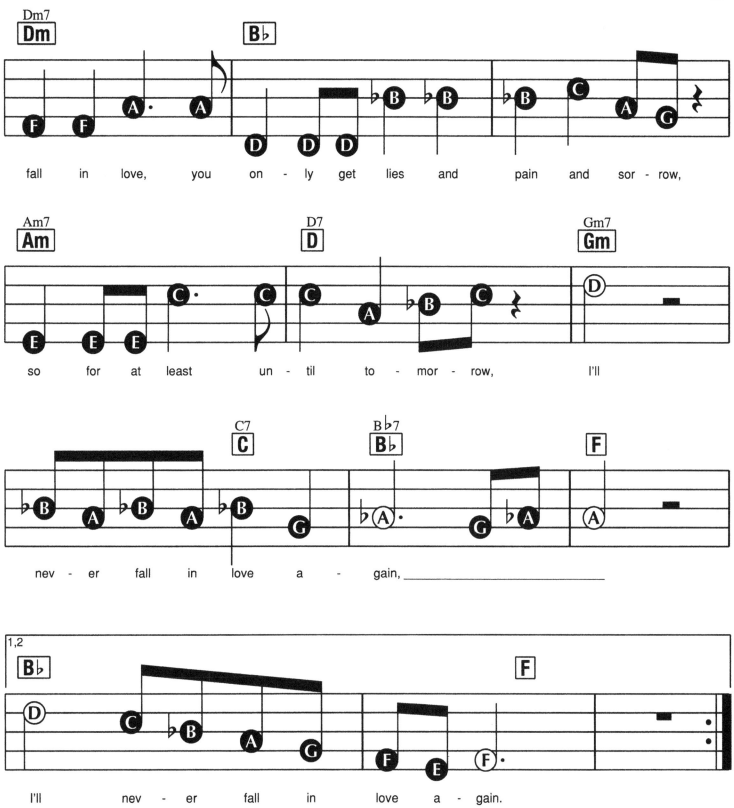

fall in love, you on - ly get lies and pain and sor - row,

so for at least un - til to - mor - row, I'll

nev - er fall in love a - gain,_____

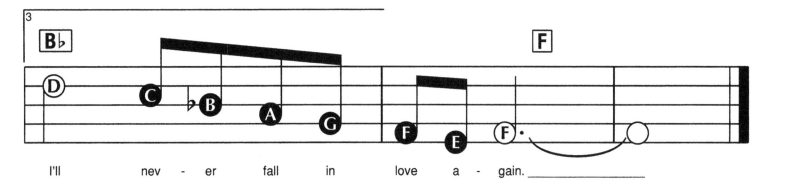

I'll nev - er fall in love a - gain.

I'll nev - er fall in love a - gain._____

The Look of Love
from CASINO ROYALE

Words by Hal David
Music by Burt Bacharach

Registration 4
Rhythm: Bossa Nova

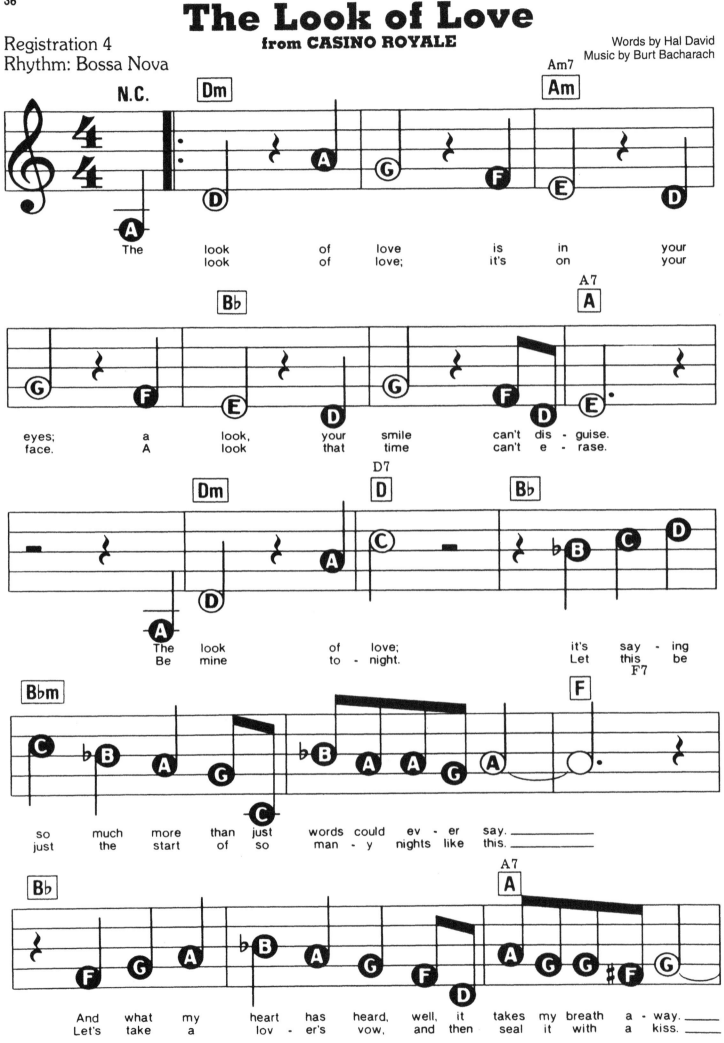

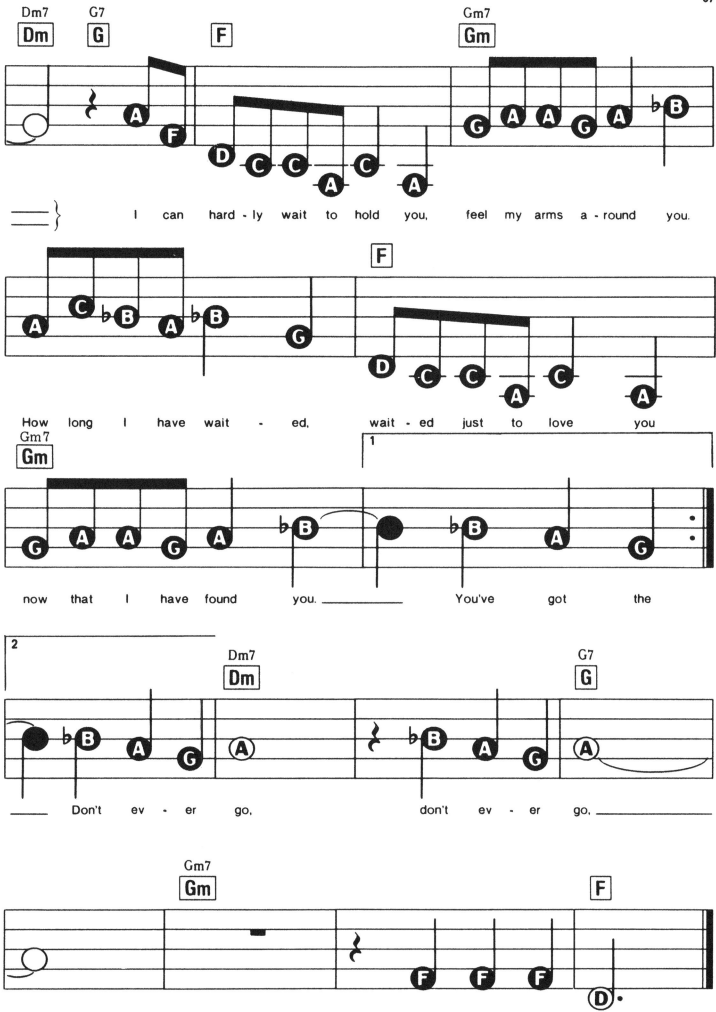

I can hard-ly wait to hold you, feel my arms a-round you.

How long I have wait-ed, wait-ed just to love you

now that I have found you. _____ You've got the

Don't ev-er go, don't ev-er go, _____

_____ I love you so.

Magic Moments

Registration 9
Rhythm: Swing or Shuffle

Lyric by Hal David
Music by Burt Bacharach

39

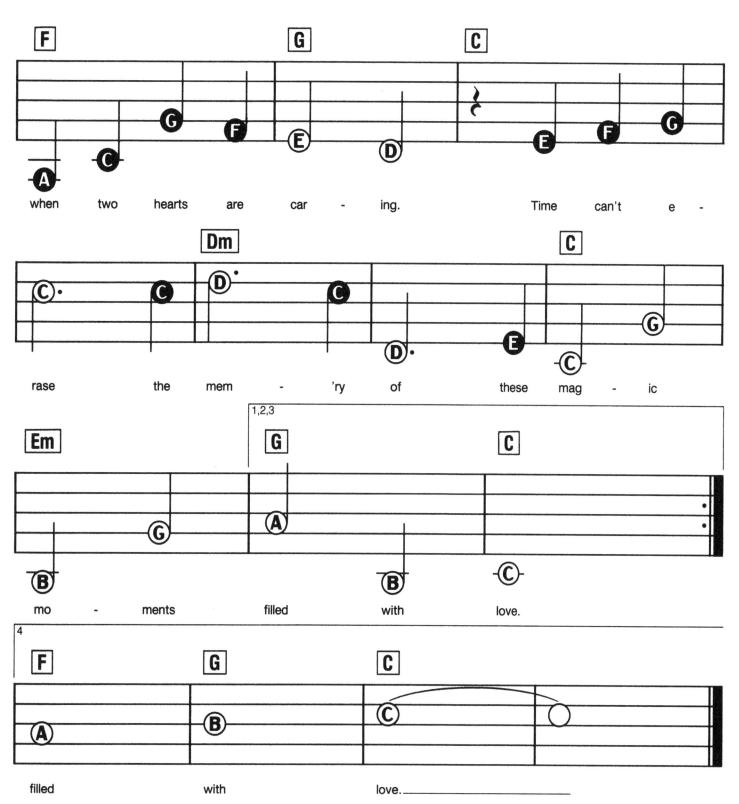

Additional Lyrics

3. The way that we cheered whenever our team was scoring a touchdown,
The time that the floor fell out of {my/your} car when {I/you} put the clutch down;
(To Chorus)

4. The penny arcade, the games that we played, the fun and the prizes,
The Halloween hop when ev'ryone came in funny disguises;
(To Chorus)

Message to Michael

Registration 9
Rhythm: Pops or Rock

Lyric by Hal David
Music by Burt Bacharach

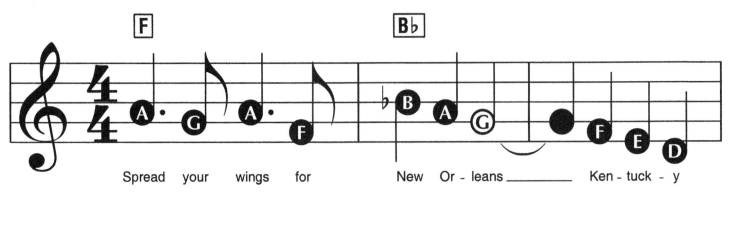

Spread your wings for New Or - leans _____ Ken - tuck - y

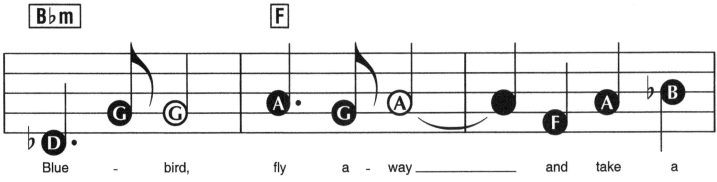

Blue - bird, fly a - way _____ and take a

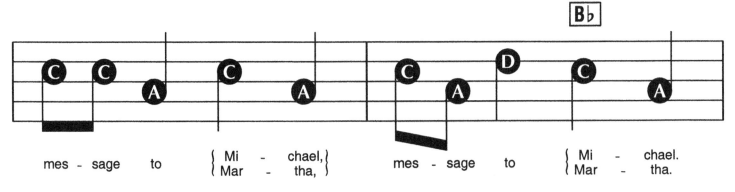

mes - sage to { Mi - chael, / Mar - tha, } mes - sage to { Mi - chael. / Mar - tha.

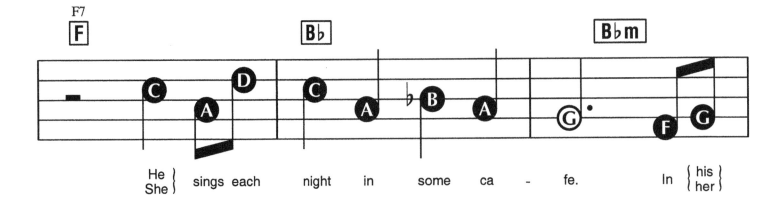

{ He / She } sings each night in some ca - fe. In { his / her }

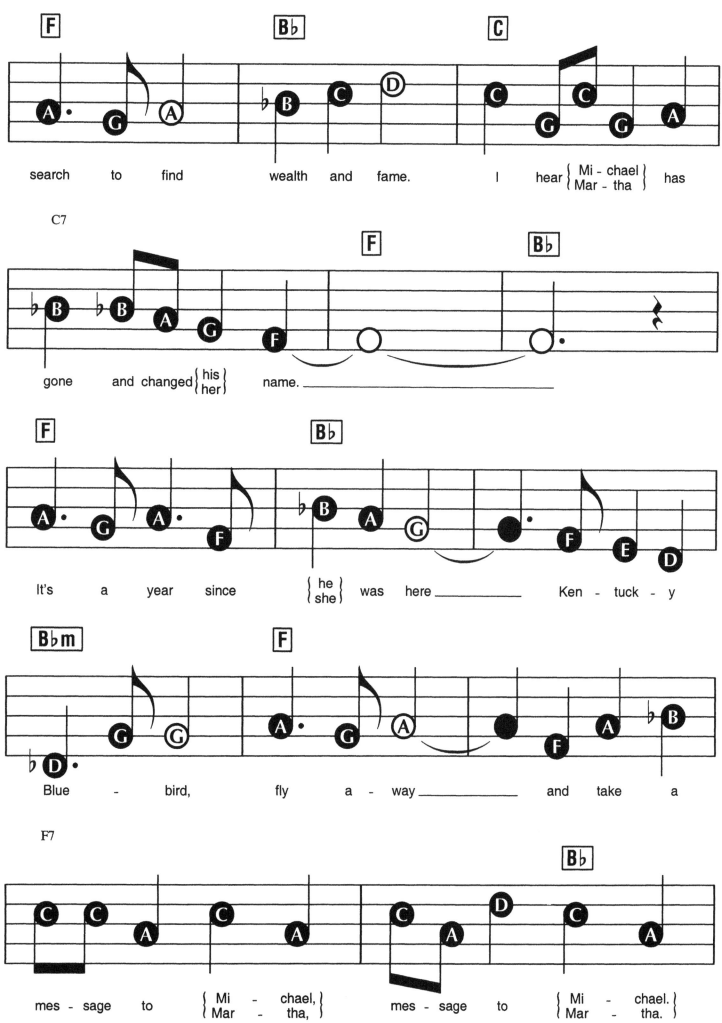

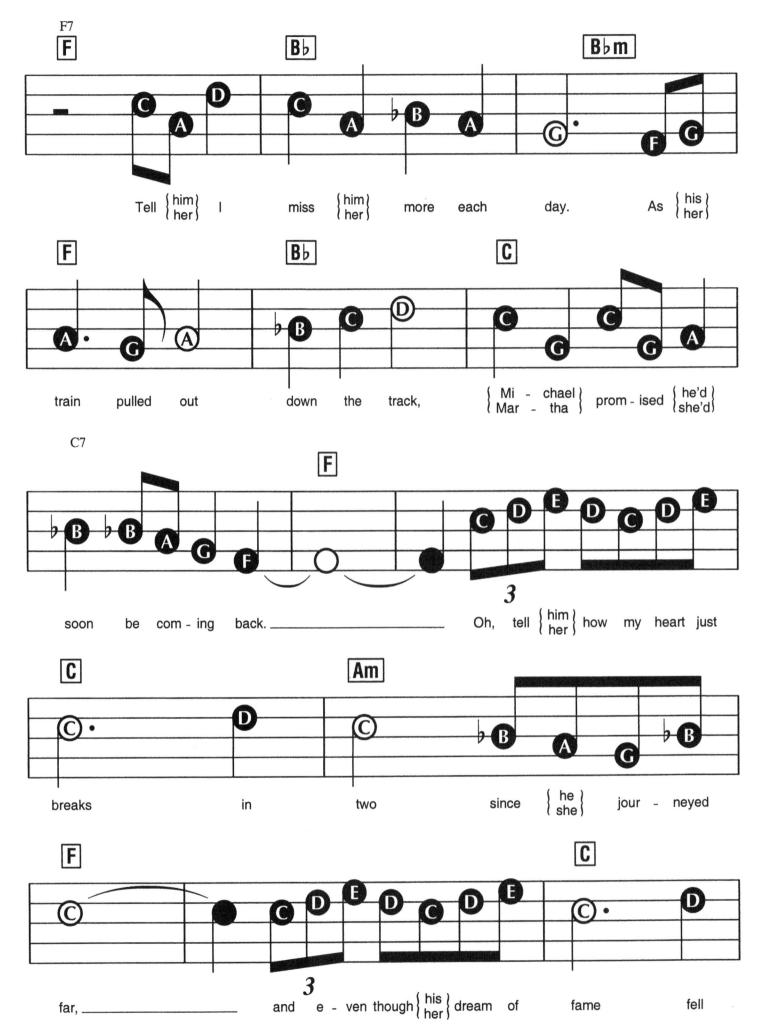

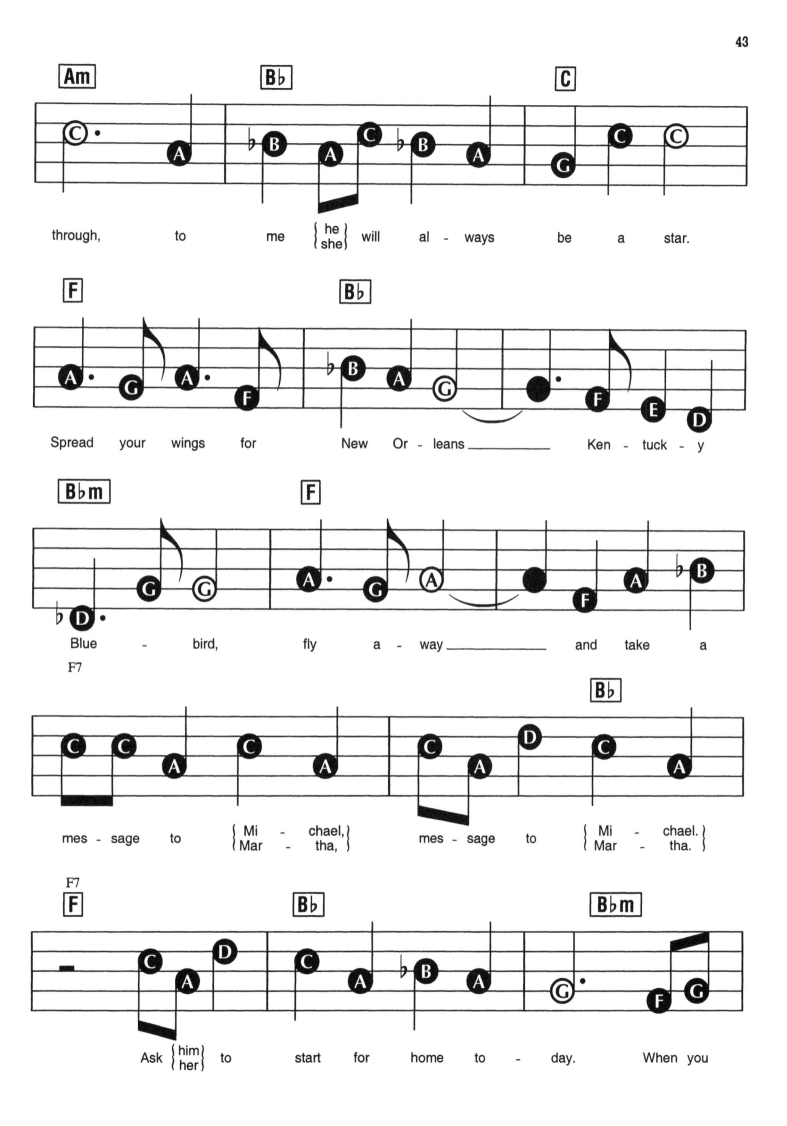

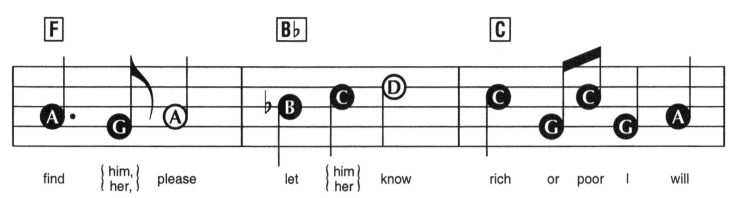

find {him, her,} please let {him her} know rich or poor I will

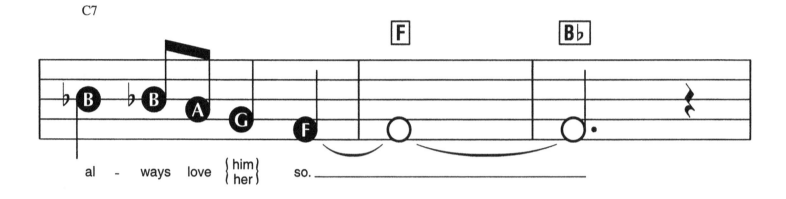

al - ways love {him her} so. _____

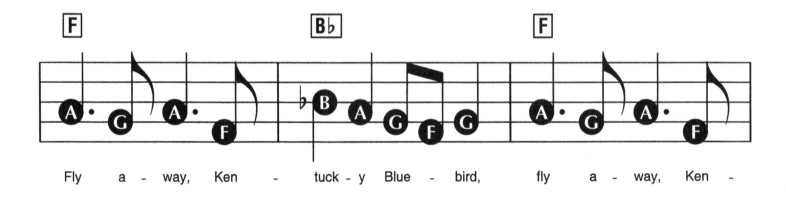

Fly a - way, Ken - tuck - y Blue - bird, fly a - way, Ken -

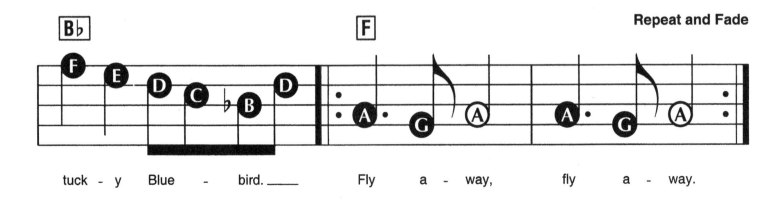

tuck - y Blue - bird. _____ Fly a - way, fly a - way.

One Less Bell to Answer

Registration 8
Rhythm: Swing Shuffle, or Fox Trot

Lyric by Hal David
Music by Burt Bacharach

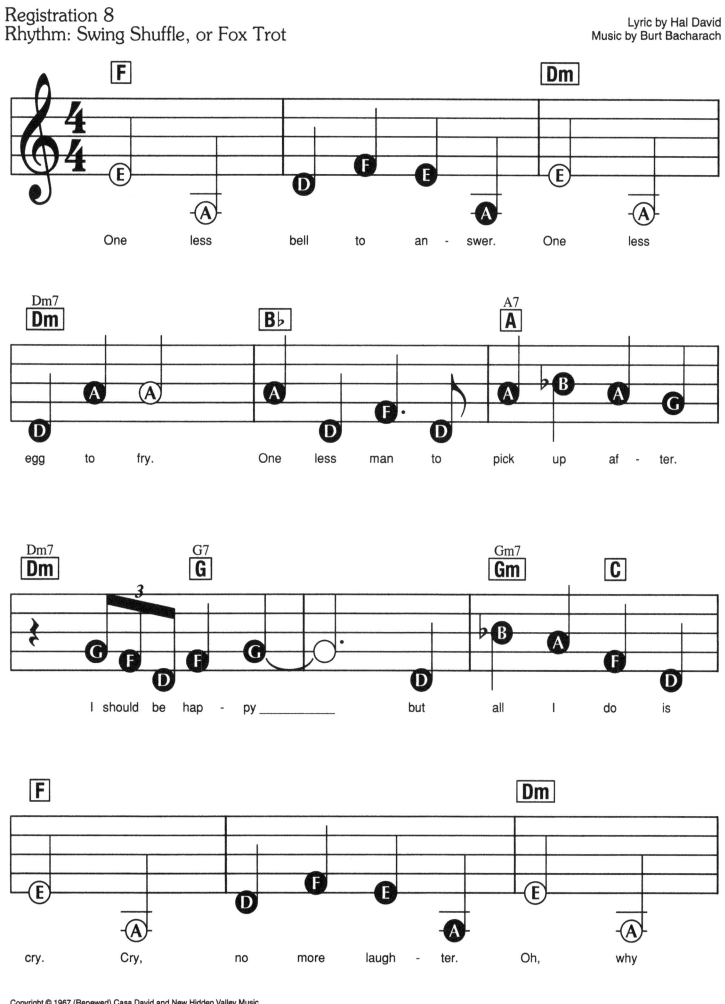

46

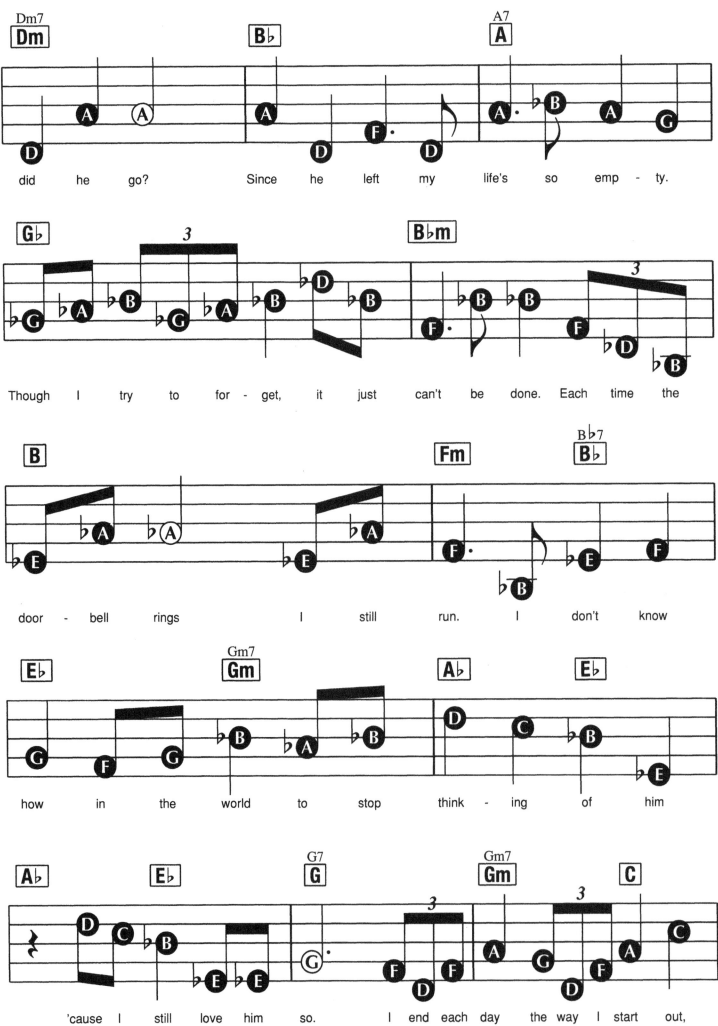

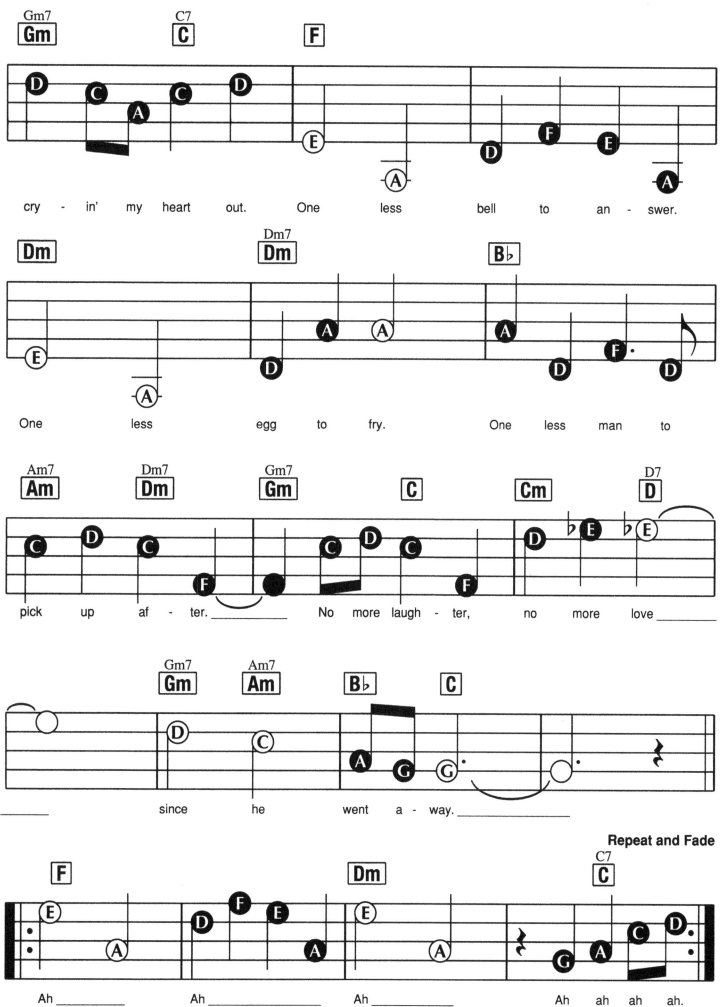

Raindrops Keep Fallin' on My Head

Registration 5
Rhythm: Swing or Shuffle

Lyric by Hal David
Music by Burt Bacharach

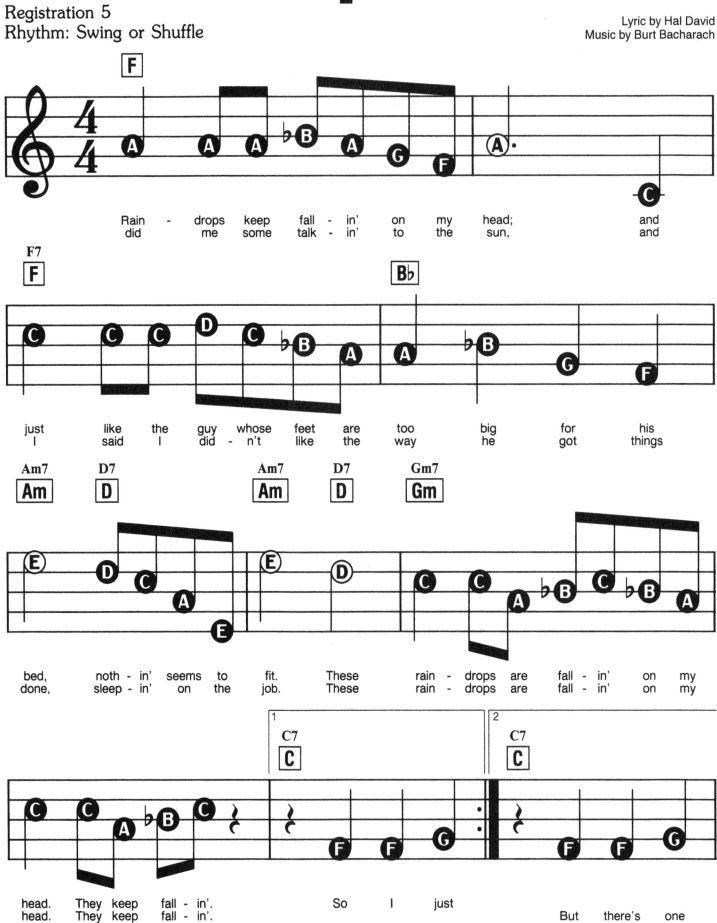

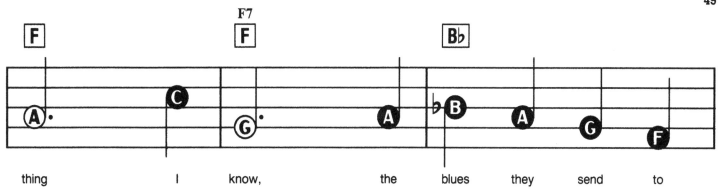

thing   I   know,   the   blues   they   send   to

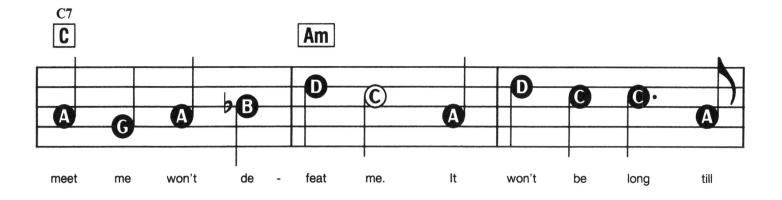

meet   me   won't   de - feat   me.   It   won't   be   long   till

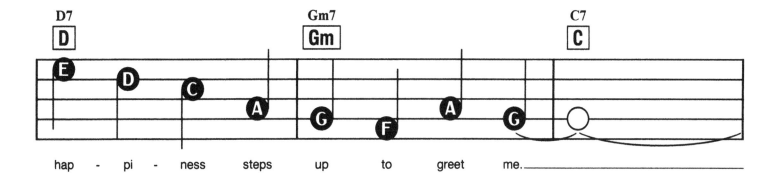

hap - pi - ness   steps   up   to   greet   me._____

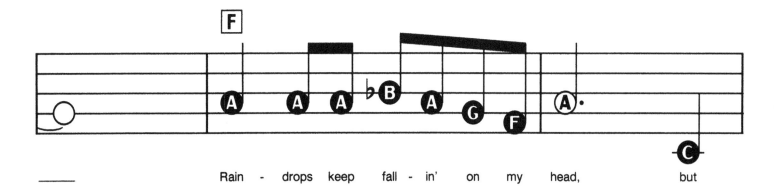

_____   Rain - drops   keep   fall - in'   on   my   head,   but

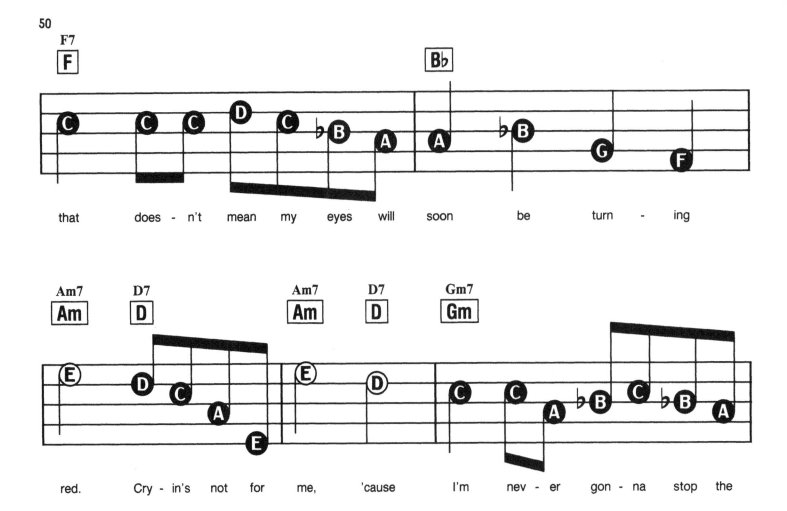

that does-n't mean my eyes will soon be turn - ing

red. Cry - in's not for me, 'cause I'm nev - er gon - na stop the

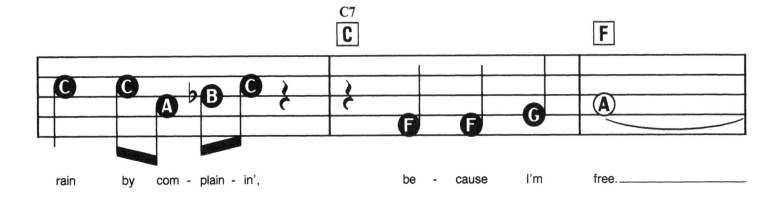

rain by com - plain - in', be - cause I'm free._____

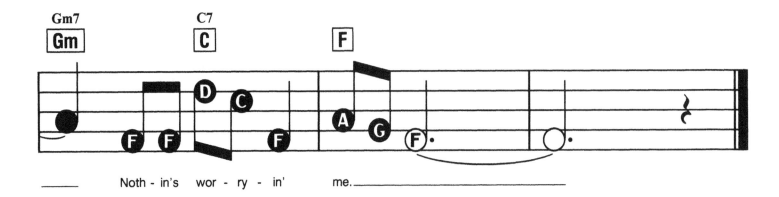

_____ Noth - in's wor - ry - in' me._____

This Guy's in Love With You

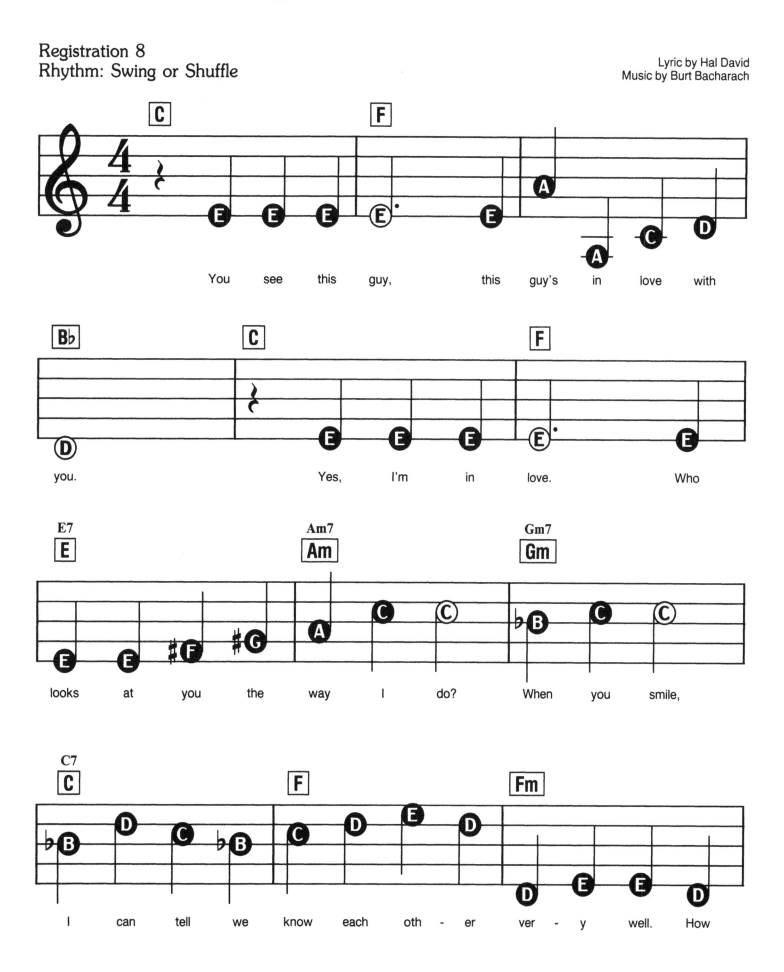

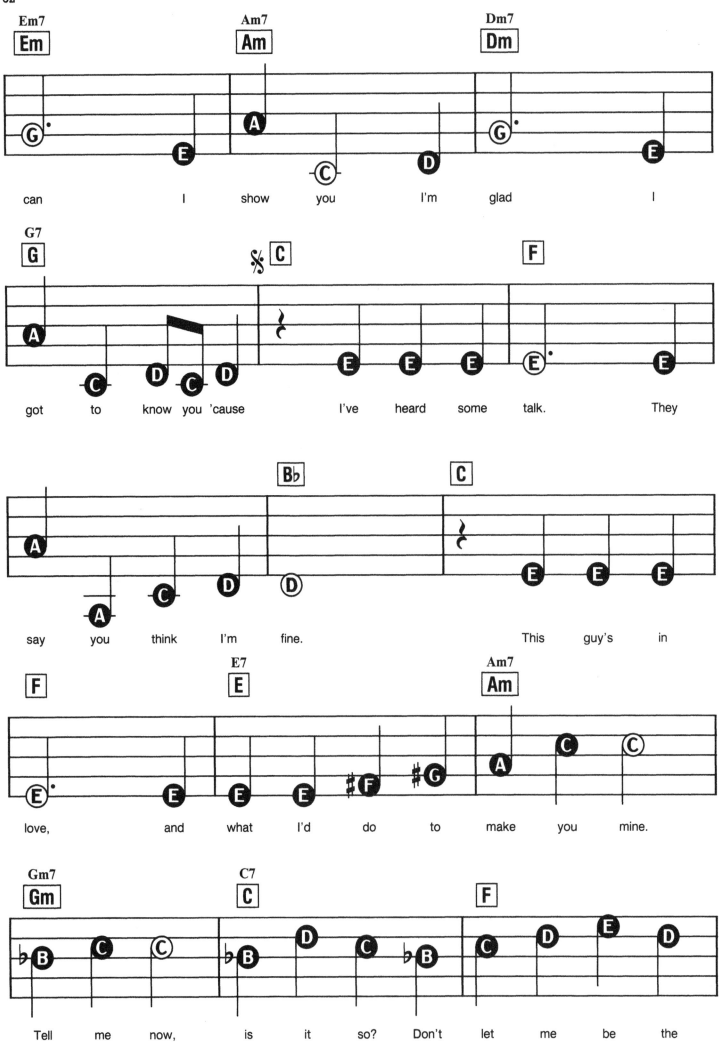

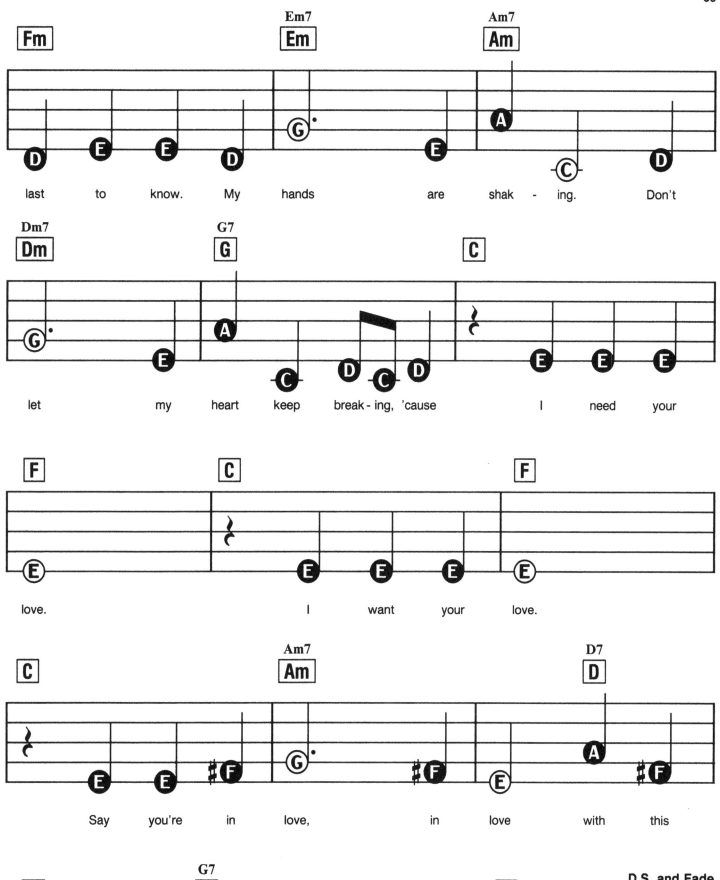

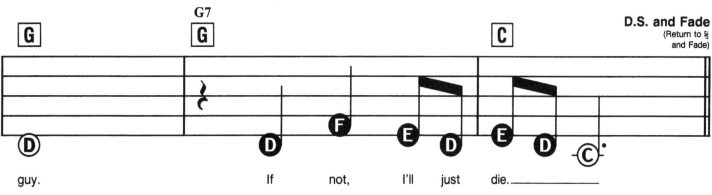

Walk on By

Registration 4
Rhythm: Rock, Pops, or Bossa Nova

Lyric by Hal David
Music by Burt Bacharach

Em7 / Em

A

B B B B B A G A B. G A G A

If you see me walk - in' down the street and I start to
I just can't get o - ver los - ing you and so if I

Em7 / Em   **A**   **Em7** / Em   **A**   **Dm7** / Dm

G #F G #F E E E D

cry each time we meet, walk on by,
seem bro - ken and blue, walk walk on by,

Em7 / Em   **Dm7** / Dm   **Em7** / Em

E E D. A A G. G

walk on by.
walk on by. Make be - lieve that
Fool - ish pride, that's

Am   **Em7** / Em

C D E F E C A A G. C

you don't see the tears, just let me grieve in
all that I have left, so let me hide in the

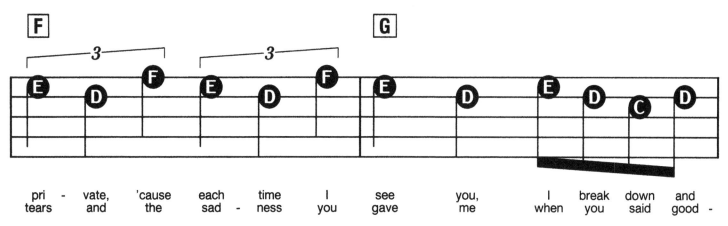

pri - vate, 'cause each time I see you, I break down and
tears and the sad - ness you gave me when you said good -

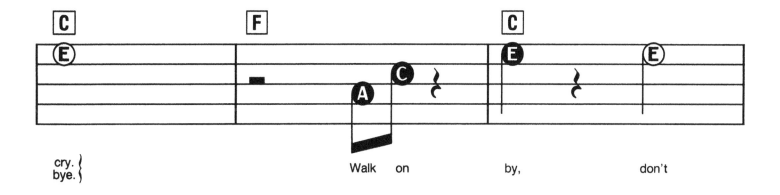

cry.
bye.

Walk on by, don't

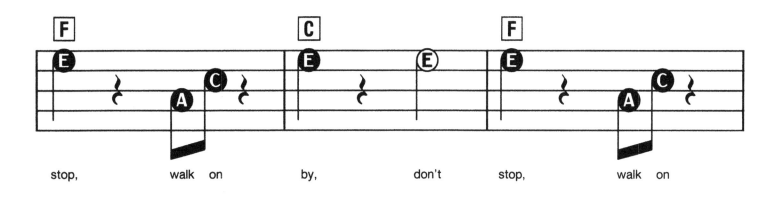

stop, walk on by, don't stop, walk on

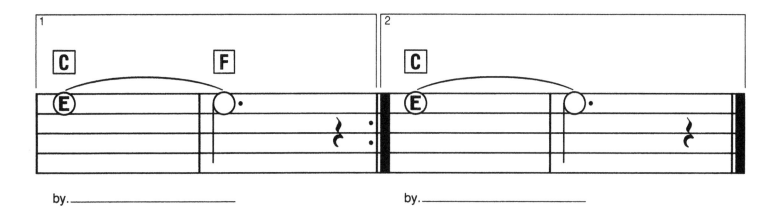

by._____ by._____

What the World Needs Now Is Love

Registration 2
Rhythm: Jazz Waltz or Waltz

Lyric by Hal David
Music by Burt Bacharach

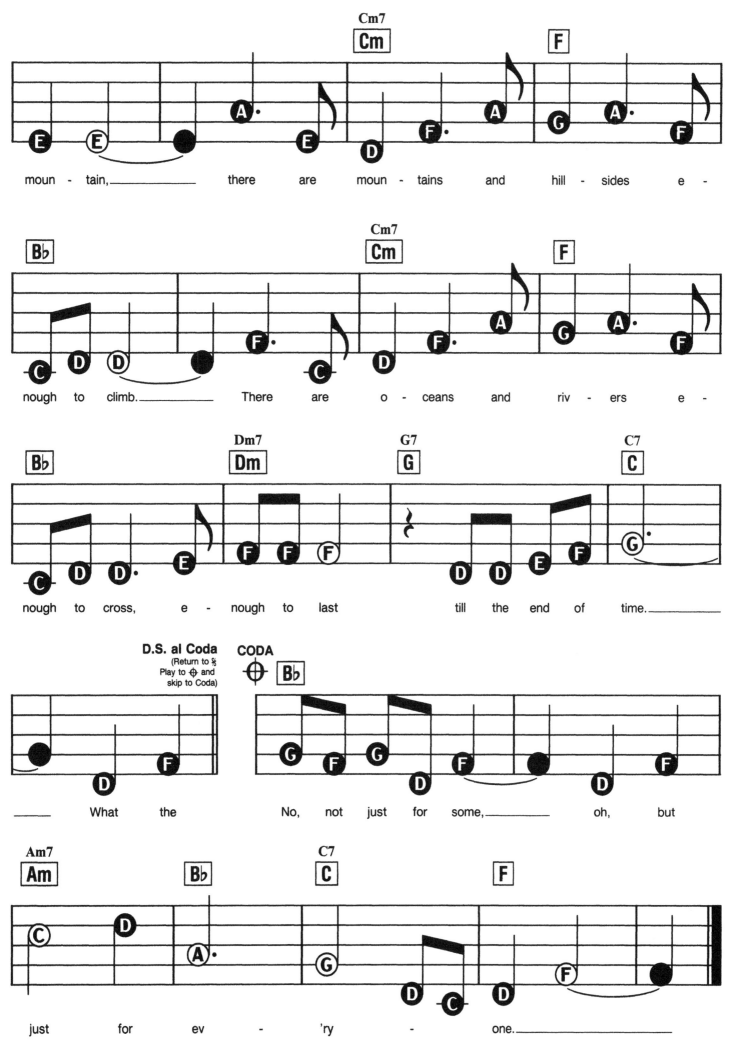

Wishin' and Hopin'

Registration 2
Rhythm: Ballad or Fox Trot

Lyric by Hal David
Music by Burt Bacharach

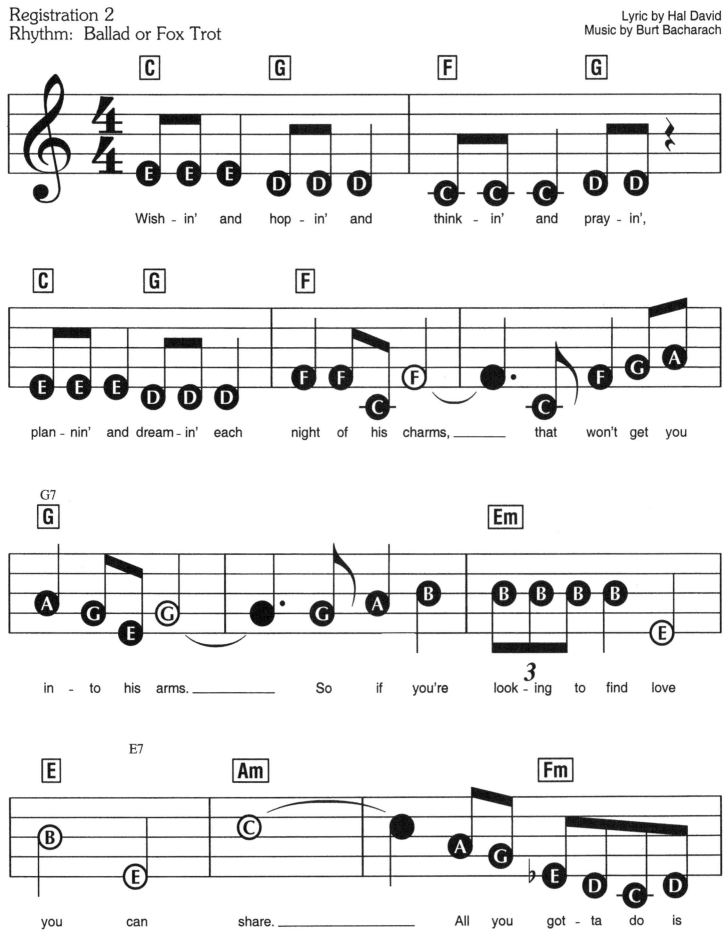

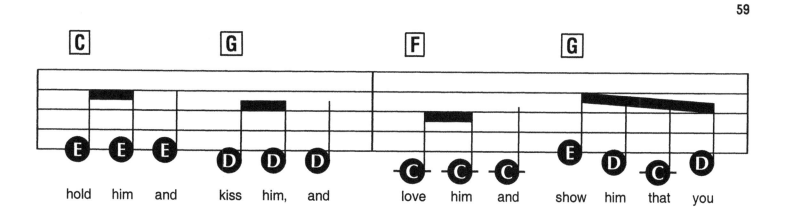
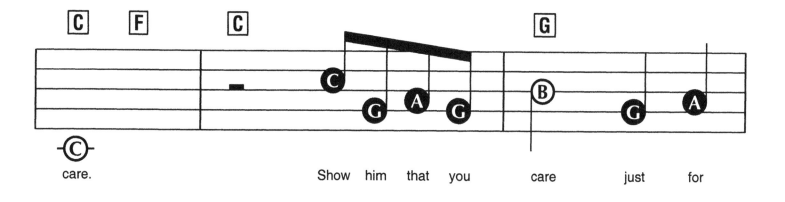
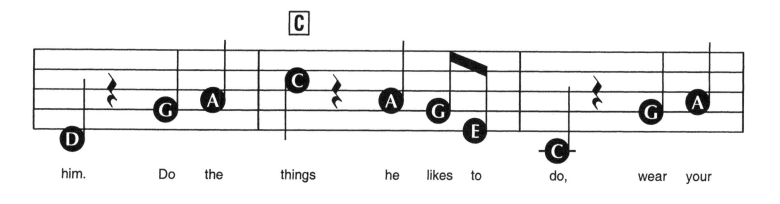
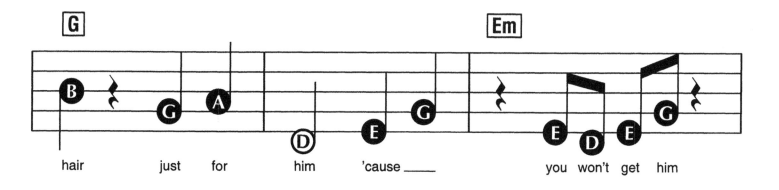

59

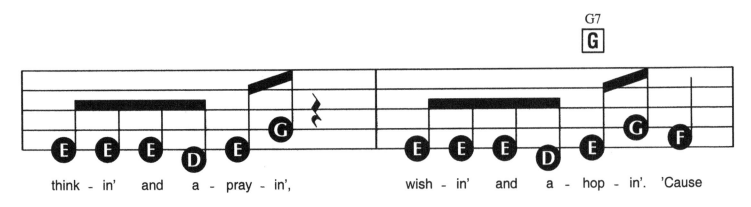

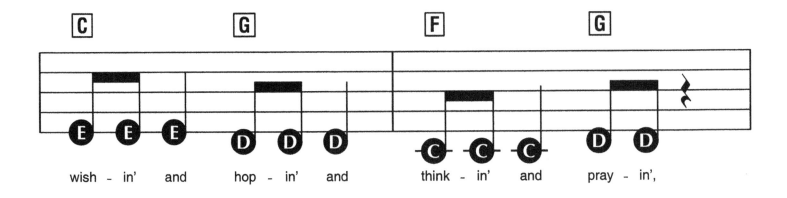

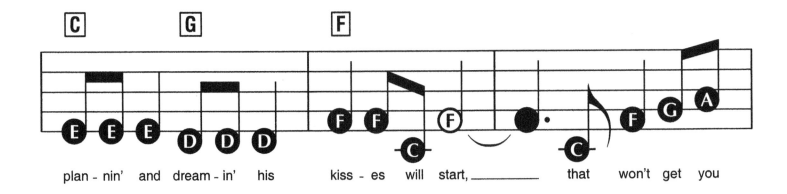

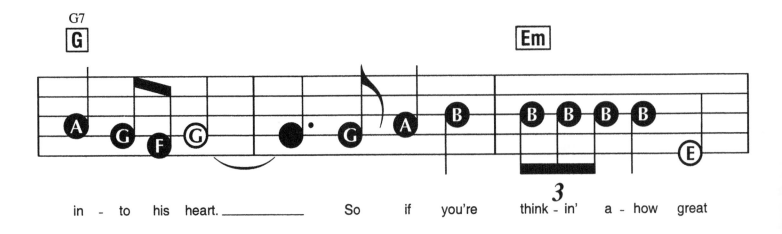

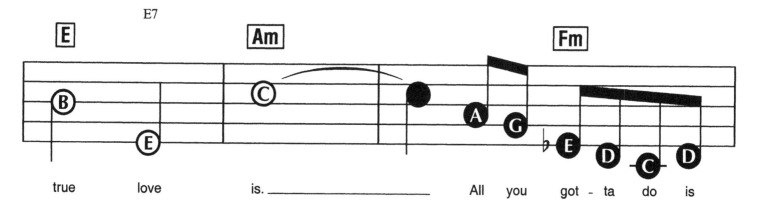

true love is. _____ All you got - ta do is

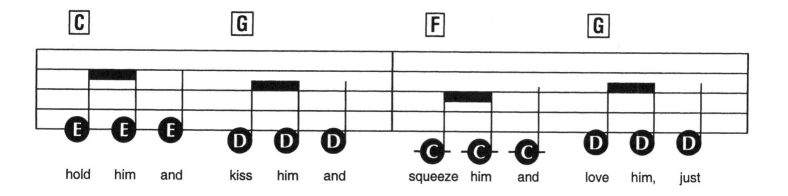

hold him and kiss him and squeeze him and love him, just

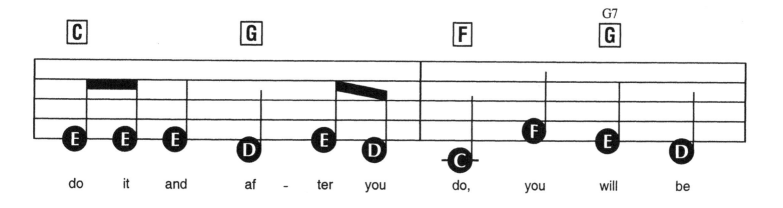

do it and af - ter you do, you will be

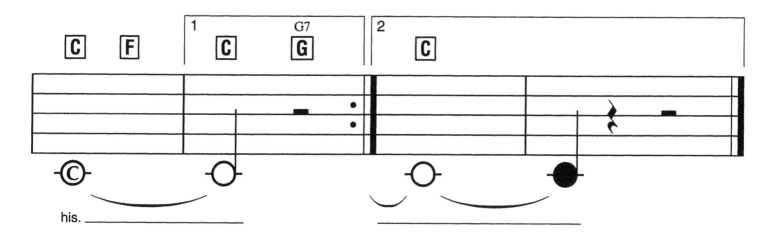

his. _____

Wives and Lovers
(Hey, Little Girl)
from the Paramount Picture WIVES AND LOVERS

Words by Hal David
Music by Burt Bacharach

Registration 1
Rhythm: Waltz or Jazz Waltz

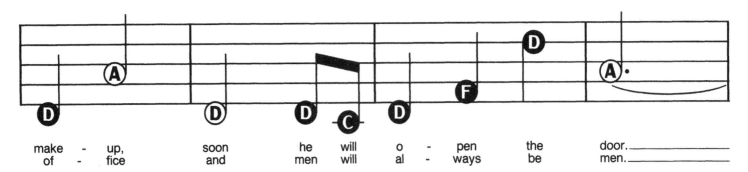

Hey,   lit - tle   girl,   comb your hair,   fix your
Day   af - ter day   there are girls   at the

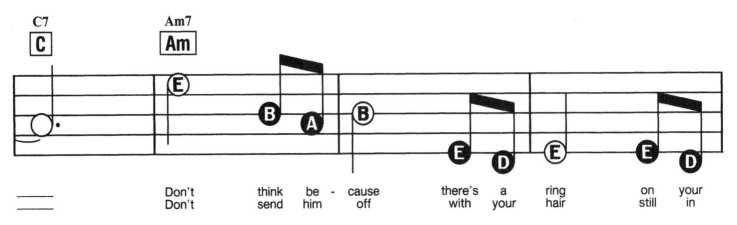

make - up,   soon   he will o - pen the door.
of - fice   and   men will al - ways be men.

Don't   think be - cause   there's a ring   on your
Don't   send him off   with your hair   still in

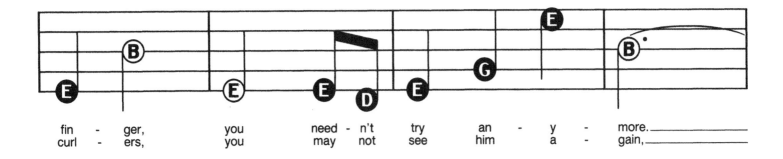

fin - ger,   you   need - n't try an - y - more.
curl - ers,   you   may not see him a - gain,

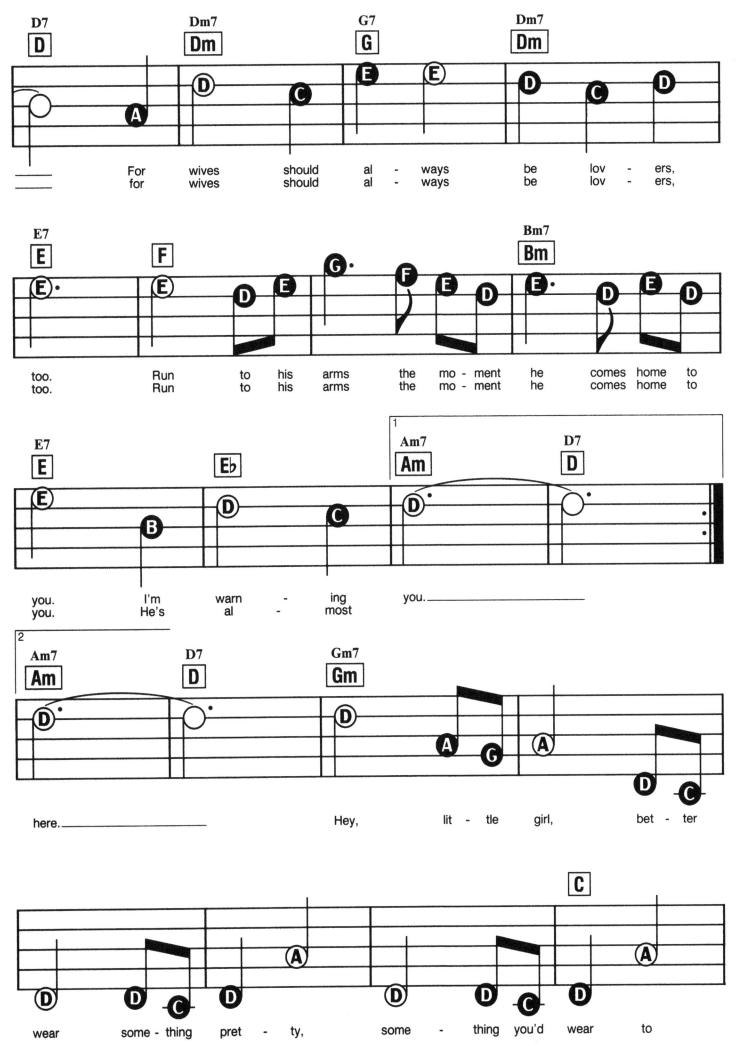